THE UNOFFICIAL **BOOK** ON

Hootsuite

The #1 Tool for Social Media Management

By Mike Allton

Printed in the United States of America

First Printing, 2014
Second Printing, 2017

The Social Media Hat
St. Louis, MO 63301

www.TheSocialMediaHat.com

Table of Contents

Forward by Martin Shervington

With brands large and small embracing social business, people often feel overwhelmed with the choices.

Unless a company has good processes in place, they simply cannot focus on what really matters - relationships. Well, imagine if you had ways to allow you to focus on the relationships that matter, instead of worrying about 'clicking the buttons'. This is what 'good tools' allow you to do.

Some people don't like the idea of using automated posting tools, but having used them on Google+ pages I can assure you the content is guaranteed to get posted where it could have been neglected otherwise. Then what? Well, it frees up myself and the team to nurture engagement and build relationships, one person at a time.

As it happens, I was a late starter on Twitter, but now Hootsuite is the tool of choice for that account. The same applies here, using automation enables the best content for my network to flow across the web; it removes the stress, the doubt and the apathy for content distribution. In turn I can 'give' by sharing more people's content having 'saved it up', generating even better relationships with the connectors. And I know it is working as I see the referral traffic coming to my website more and more.

Then there are the daily processes, the list building, the circle building and the message sending. This is all about relationships, and in time those will turn into business opportunities. You'll need to be organized though, as without this you are just throwing content out there and not picking up that every 'click' someone makes is an indication of interest and an opportunity for you to engage and build the relationship further.

Then we have the people running the accounts, the personalities behind the brand pages. Whether it is Plus Your Business client accounts or my own, the same applies. You need to consider the brand positioning, values and metrics by which the accounts will be judged. If you are a social media manager reading this, then know that people love people; let go a little, be present, be you and allow the world to fall in love with the brands you represent.

Together the tools, processes, and the people all will work together to build engagement and referral traffic to your website, whilst making people feel special along the way.

Martin Shervington, April 2014
www.MartinShervington.com

Introduction

When I started using Hootsuite years ago, I had the same misperceptions about social media that many of us do when first starting. I thought I could use social networks as advertising platforms for whatever I was selling. The idea of being able to plug an update into a tool that would blast it out to multiple social networks at the same time was appealing.

It took me a while to see how futile that really was for marketing my business.

But as I learned and evolved, I also began to see far more value and benefits from using tools like Hootsuite. At the same time, it occurred to me that this tool in particular was *really* complicated! I was finding ways to automate the tasks that *should* be automated, and easing the tasks that needed easing, but getting there was a challenge.

How should I be organizing my tabs? What should I have in my streams? How can I schedule updates for specific times and dates so that my activity is better scheduled?

These were the questions I was running up against regular, and like any good blogger, started to document my questions *and* the answers that I discovered. That process turned into a series of extremely popular blog posts, and those were the basis of this book.

While most of the chapters correspond to specific blog posts and articles, and a lot of the information is the same – a great deal of time has been invested to ensure that all of the information is current as of this publishing, and that even more information was added wherever possible.

Chapters have been expanded, more screenshots and instructions have been included, and additional chapters have been added.

The result is a book which, I think you'll agree, can serve as a complete guide and resource for not only how to use Hootsuite, but also how to be successful on social media in general, with Hootsuite helping you to get there.

I hope you learn as much from reading this as I learned from writing it. Stay tuned at the end for some additional resources and information, and a special invitation to join my online community.

Mike Allton, April 2014
www.TheSocialMediaHat.com

About Hootsuite

I promise not to bore you with a history lesson about Hootsuite, but there are some facts and information about the business that I think you'll find interesting.

Hootsuite was started in 2008 by a group of developers who wanted to create a better social media experience. Hootsuite is led by founder and CEO Ryan Holmes, and now boasts more than 9 million users. Among all social media management tools, Hootsuite is by far the most popular and most highly recommended.

A college drop-out, Holmes started a paintball company and pizza restaurant before founding Invoke Media, the company that developed Hootsuite in 2009.

Invoke had created software for businesses to run contests online. Companies utilizing the software began asking for social media support backing their contests. It was in providing this support that Invoke saw a need for a management tool that would help clients avoid having to continuously log in and out of various social media accounts and prevent team members from stepping on each other's toes.

In September, 2008 the Hootsuite concept was drawn out and the product launched later that fall. What started off as a three-man project within Invoke quickly turned into something bigger. Everyone involved realised the potential and popularity of this new tool and within only a year (October 2009), Hootsuite was incorporated and separated from Invoke. By November of 2010, 1 million people across the globe were using Hootsuite and the company's growth has quickened ever since.

Hootsuite is a preferred, certified partner of Facebook, Twitter, LinkedIn and Google+, and features apps within the App Directory for YouTube, Instagram, Pinterest, Tumblr and more.

In the coming chapters, we going to explore how to use this tool and maximize our time so that our social media activity is both efficient and effective.

Let's get started!

Getting Started in Hootsuite

Why Hootsuite

I have extolled the benefits of Hootsuite on a number of occasions, but it's probably a good idea to run through the Greatest Hits here so you'll be motivated to keep reading.

First and foremost, Hootsuite supports brand and company pages for your business   on Facebook, Twitter, LinkedIn and Google+ (while   Twitter doesn't have a separate business account type, it's common to create a company account along with personal accounts to represent CEOs, business owners and employees). That makes Hootsuite the ideal tool for an active business who has a presence on all of the major networks.

Second, Hootsuite provides a robust sharing and scheduling tool. With Hootsuite, business owners and designated team members can craft a post, include a shortened link, and even attach a photo. They can choose which networks to share it to, and share the post immediately or at a scheduled date and time. Hootsuite even includes an Auto Schedule feature that will space out posts and publish them at optimum times.

Third, Hootsuite includes the option to actually set up teams and members. For larger organizations, this allows for a much greater degree of flexibility and usability for social media management. Certain teams can be granted access to select accounts, and team members can share social media activity, like direct messages, with other team members for action.

Finally, Hootsuite offers a rich set of metrics for analysis of the impact of your social media activity. This is an area we're going to dig into a lot more, as measuring your results should be a critical aspect of your social media strategy.

Get Started

If you haven't yet signed up for a Hootsuite account, you can get a <u>free 30-day trial of Hootsuite Pro here</u>. Once you've signed up, make sure that you also download the appropriate app for mobile access to your account and functionality. [<u>iTunes</u> | <u>Android</u>]

Which plan should you choose? The free plan is actually fine for most users, as it supports up to three social networks and two RSS feeds. So, if you want to use Hootsuite to manage your two branded profiles, and perhaps a personal Twitter account, it will be great.

The Pro plan adds support for up to 50 social networks. The networks supported are the same for both plans, just the total number of connected networks. Since I have both personal and branded accounts on all the networks, I use Pro. I also connected key LinkedIn Groups.

Hootsuite also offers an Enterprise package that includes an unlimited number of social networks, far more users, education and support, and other features.

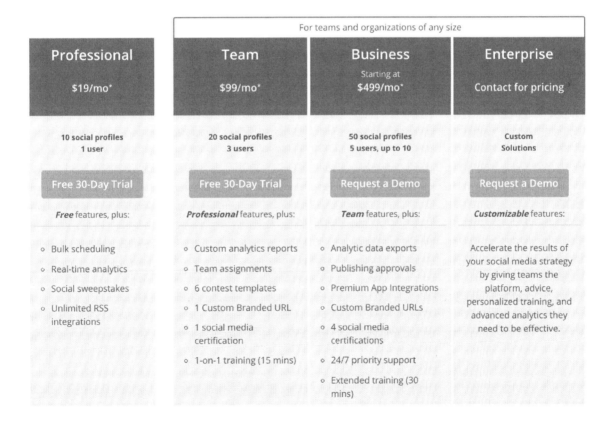

Professional	Team	Business	Enterprise
		For teams and organizations of any size	
$19/mo*	$99/mo*	Starting at $499/mo*	Contact for pricing
10 social profiles 1 user	20 social profiles 3 users	50 social profiles 5 users, up to 10	Custom Solutions
Free 30-Day Trial	Free 30-Day Trial	Request a Demo	Request a Demo
Free features, plus:	*Professional* features, plus:	*Team* features, plus:	*Customizable* features:
○ Bulk scheduling	○ Custom analytics reports	○ Analytic data exports	Accelerate the results of your social media strategy by giving teams the platform, advice, personalized training, and advanced analytics they need to be effective.
○ Real-time analytics	○ Team assignments	○ Publishing approvals	
○ Social sweepstakes	○ 6 contest templates	○ Premium App Integrations	
○ Unlimited RSS integrations	○ 1 Custom Branded URL	○ Custom Branded URLs	
	○ 1 social media certification	○ 4 social media certifications	
	○ 1-on-1 training (15 mins)	○ 24/7 priority support	
		○ Extended training (30 mins)	

Once you have selected the plan that you wish to use, and I would encourage you to take advantage of the free trial, the first thing to do is to begin connecting your accounts. For each social network, you will need to authorize Hootsuite to access that account and post on your behalf. For Facebook, LinkedIn and Google+, once you connect the account you will be asked to choose which profile, page or group you want to connect.

To add more connections, click on your profile image in the upper left corner, or go to https://Hootsuite.com/dashboard#/member. Click on the Add a Social Network button and select the network you want to add. In addition to Twitter, Facebook, Google+ and LinkedIn, Hootsuite supports Instagram, WordPress and YouTube. Additional networks like Flickr or Vimeo or Pinterest can also be added via Apps, which we'll cover in more detail later on.

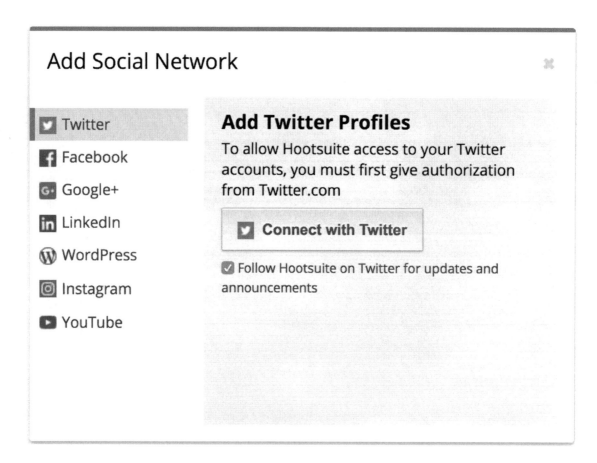

In the next chapter, we'll cover Hootsuite Tabs and Streams; how to set them up and some best practices and options. We're also going to be talking about scheduling and automation, twitter chats, crafting posts, reports and more, so keep reading!

How to Set Up Tabs & Streams

Tabs and Streams

The Hootsuite dashboard is a dense tool, which makes it somewhat intimidating to new users. The interface can be packed with information and updates, so it takes some getting used to. Hopefully this chapter and the rest of the book will help you become more familiar with Hootsuite, and thereby get more value out of your use of the tool.

The dashboard is divided into tabs, and each tab can contain streams.

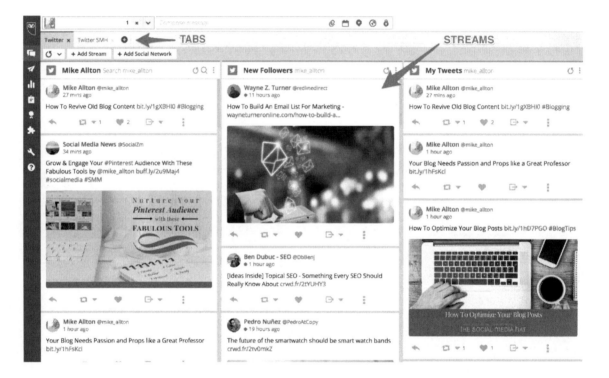

A Basic Hootsuite account can add a maximum of 20 tabs per dashboard. A typical example of a tab would be for your Twitter account.

Within each tab, you can set up streams to monitor different kinds of information and activity. A Basic Hootsuite account can have a maximum of 10 streams per tab. A typical example of a stream would be one that displays your Mentions within your Twitter account.

Tab Setup

When you first get started with Hootsuite and begin connecting social networks, each network will get its own Tab by default. While this may ultimately be the way you want your tabs to be organized, know that you can edit them, move them around, rename them, and add more.

To rename a tab, click the tab and then click the tab name again. This will allow you to edit the tab name. Particularly once you've added a number of tabs, you'll likely want to adjust the tab names to be shorter and more meaningful for easier navigation.

To move tabs around, simply select and drag the tab you want to move.

To add a new tab, look for the + button to the right of your last tab.

Once clicked, you'll be able to name your new tab and then add whatever streams you wish.

Stream Setup

So, once you have one or more tabs, it's time to set up some streams. If you're dividing your tabs by social network, you'll most likely want to assign streams within each tab to monitor your posts for comments and activity, messages sent to you through that network, and other social actions your followers may take. The available stream options will vary from network to network.

Twitter - Home Feed, Mentions, Direct Messages (Inbox or Outbox), Sent Tweets, Favorite Tweets, ReTweets, Scheduled Tweets, Searches, Keywords, Lists

Facebook - News Feed (Most Recent, Status Updates, Photos, Videos - all can be filtered by specific Friends or Fans), Wall Posts, Events, Scheduled Messages, Search

LinkedIn - My Updates, All Updates, All Discussions, Most Popular Discussions, Company Updates, Scheduled Updates, Job Search

Google+ - Home Stream, Sent Messages, Circle Stream (filtered by selected

Circle), Scheduled Messages, Search

As mentioned earlier, you can set up as many as 10 streams per tab, so you can make sure that you're monitoring your activity and your followers activity on all your accounts.

Tab & Stream Options

Certainly, you can go with the default tabs for each network and typical monitoring streams within each. One of the powerful features within Hootsuite is the option to create saved searches as streams.

You might include one or more within each network tab, or set up new tabs for specific searches and have the different networks as streams within each.

Lead Generation

For instance, businesses should be monitoring keywords on social networks for opportunities to inject themselves into conversations, answer questions, and create relationships. I might set up a saved search on "Help with Blogging" and regularly check it for people who are actively asking for help with their blogging and content marketing. I can set up a **Blogging Help** tab and then create streams within it with saved searched on the networks I want to monitor, particularly Twitter and Google+, where most posts are Public.

Social Listening

Businesses and *personal brands* should also set up one or more tabs with streams to monitor networks for references of their name. This is referred to as Social Listening, and gives brands an option to respond to negative comments, or show appreciation for positive support.

Clients and Influencers

Part of the strategy for using Social Media to create and strengthen your relationship with clients, potential clients and influencers is making an effort to connect with and engage them. How do you do that? By following or circling them, paying attention to what they're talking about, and chiming it at appropriate times. You might, for instance, set up a Circle on Google+ for influencers in your industry and set that up as a filtered stream. It would allow you to see what they're posting and talking about and comment.

Since you can set up as many as 20 tabs, be creative! Set up different tabs for different purposes, and use your streams to feed you and your dashboard the information you're looking for.

In the next chapter, we're going to cover how to create your first post within Hootsuite to your social networks, and how to use the built in scheduling options.

How to Craft and Schedule Social Media Posts using Hootsuite

Creating a Post

The Hootsuite Dashboard includes a powerful Compose Message tool that allows you to craft a message and share it with selected social networks. You'll find it in the upper left corner of the dashboard on the web, or by tapping the compose icon at the top of the mobile app.

You'll typically begin by typing in or pasting the text that you want to share. If you have a link, copy and paste it into the URL field on the web and click the Shrink button to turn the full link into a shortened link. Or, on mobile, paste the link into the compose field and then tap the Shrink Links button under the Menu. This will not only shorten your link to use fewer characters, but also use the ow.ly shortened link format which will allow you to track link clicks via Hootsuite's analytics. I'll often use Hootsuite shortened links even if I'm putting the links somewhere other than a social media post.

You can include multiple links if you want to, but it's recommended that you include no more than one link per post. You can and should make good use of hashtags, since Twitter, Google+ and Facebook all support hashtags. And while LinkedIn does not, I believe it's only a matter of time before they do, so I don't worry if one of my posts to LinkedIn includes hashtags. Some day they may work!

> *Hashtags are any combination of letters and/or numbers preceded by the pound sign (#). Social Networks that support hashtags will automatically convert them into links to other posts using the same exact hashtag. This allows* your *post to be found by people interested*

in a particular hashtag, even if they aren't already following you.

To the left of the Compose Message box is the Social Network Selector. Using the drop down list, you can choose from any social networks that you've set up. As you select networks, their individual icons will appear in the selected network area. You can click on any of the selected thumbnails to deselect that network. Also, as you select networks, you will see a character count at the bottom of the Compose Message box, letting you know if you're reaching character limits for Twitter, LinkedIn or Facebook posts.

If you have a link in your post and select to share that to Facebook, LinkedIn or Google+, Hootsuite will automatically bring up the Preview box. The Preview will show you the rich snippet that can appear on those networks, and includes a Title, Description and Image, if the linked article provides them. If more than one image is detected, you can scroll through the results to choose the best one. You can also edit the Title and Description as needed, prior to posting. If the preview doesn't look good at all, you can X it closed and share the update without a preview. Whatever text and link is in the Compose Message box is all that will be shared.

Scheduling a Post

When you've created a post and selected one or more social networks, you can either send it immediately, or schedule it to be shared later. When scheduling, you have three options: Select Date, Auto Schedule and Bulk Schedule.

Select Date

Click on the calendar icon to open the Scheduling dialogue box.

Here, you can select a specific date on the calendar, followed by a specific time. That's straightforward enough, but there are a couple of added features Hootsuite provides.

First, if you're not sure what else you might have scheduled to post around the time you want to share this new post, click on the "View date in Publisher" button. This will switch the background from whatever you were looking at (presumably streams) to the Publisher view. It keeps your post intact, and allows you to look at your Hootsuite calendar and see what else you have scheduled to be shared. You can then adjust the share date and time as needed and schedule it.

Second, if you need or want confirmation that a post has gone out, you can check the "Email me when message is sent" box, and receive an email confirmation after the post goes out.

AutoSchedule

One of the more powerful options within Hootsuite is AutoSchedule. AutoSchedule is activated by clicking on the Scheduler icon and turning AutoSchedule on. From that point forward, until you turn it off, any post you share will automatically be AutoScheduled. AutoSchedule does two things for you really well.

First, when you've finished crafting your post, you can allow Hootsuite to share it at the most optimum time. According to Hootsuite CEO Ryan Holmes, "It's really quite simple--instead of our users manually selecting what time they want to schedule or post their social media messages using our Scheduling feature, they can opt to use our new AutoSchedule technology to optimize and automate the scheduling process. We want our users spending more time finding and sharing content and less time worrying about the best time of day to share it." The tool uses algorithms to determine the best time to post, per network, and schedules your post to take advantage of that timeframe.

Second, when you AutoSchedule a post to more than one network, Hootsuite will stagger the posts at least 15 minutes apart, making sure that you don't spam the same post to multiple networks at the same time if you don't need to.

When you want to share a post immediately, or schedule it for a specific time, turn AutoSchedule off and then proceed to share your post.

Hootsuite has also recently added the ability to customize AutoSchedule behavior by adding:

- An adjustable limit to the number of AutoScheduled posts per day
- Select which days of the week can be scheduled
- Select a window of time during the day for posts

So, by going into Settings and selecting AutoSchedule, you can choose to allow up to 4 AutoScheduled posts per day, Monday through Friday, from 8AM until 5PM. These scheduling parameters apply to all social profiles and users currently.

Bulk Schedule

The final scheduling option is to Bulk Schedule posts. This feature allows you to create a spreadsheet offline and then upload it, creating up to 50 posts at a time. The spreadsheet can indicate the date and time of each post, the text to share, and a link to be shortened. When you upload your spreadsheet, you can choose multiple networks just as when crafting an individual post.

The bulk scheduler is a great way to make sure that you're regularly sharing key business information or evergreen articles. Due to the fact that the method only supports text and link posts, it's best suited for Twitter accounts. I will be digging into the details and techniques of bulk scheduling in a future post.

Regardless of which method you use to schedule your posts, you can always go to the Publisher tab to view your upcoming posts. Keep this in mind if you ever need to edit or cancel a scheduled post. Just go to Publisher, find the post, and click on the Edit button, which you can use to change the content of the post or the date it's scheduled.

Additional Posting Information

When posting to Facebook or Twitter or Google+, you can attach full images to your posts, just as if you'd shared an image on that network. Begin crafting your post as usual, and when you're ready, drag an image from your desktop into the Compose Message tool. The image will be attached and you will see a new shortened URL in the message box. If you simply want the image displayed on the post, leave the box checked which will hide the image URL and not include it in the text of your update. We will dig into this feature more in the next chapter, as it is a particularly powerful option.

If you regularly share posts from Hootsuite to the same social networks, you can "pin" them so that they'll be selected by default each time you start a new message. While in the Compose Message box, open the social network selector, mouse over the network you want to choose, and click on the pin button, all the way to right, just to the left of the social network icon. To unselect, just repeat and click on pin again.

If you're regularly choosing from a select number of accounts to share to, try marking them as favorites and changing your social network selector to only show favorites. You will see the Favorite toggle on each accounts entry, right next to the Pin toggle. If, like me, you've connected quite a few LinkedIn Groups and other Pages that you may not regularly post to, this can make it far easier to get to the brand accounts you use more regularly.

The network selector also includes All and Clear buttons which are used to select every social network you have set up, or clear out all that you've chosen. Note that you cannot share a post to more than 5 networks at a time unless it is scheduled. You can also start typing a network profile name in the selector box and Hootsuite will attempt to auto complete the account for you.

If you're crafting a post to share and you realize that you want to share it to a social network that you have not yet connected, you can click the + button right on the network selector tool to add a new network on the fly, keeping your in-progress message completely intact.

If you want to include your location on supported status updates, you can do so easily. While crafting your status update, click the Location button along the bottom of the Compose Message box. You will be prompted to allow Hootsuite to detect your location, and then your current location will appear at the bottom of the Compose Message box.

If you find that you're sharing the same update on a regular basis, you can save it as a template! Compose the update once, and then click on the floppy disk icon at the bottom of the Compose Message box. You'll need to have one social network selected, though you'll be able to pick and choose different networks when you recall the template. Then, later, you can click the arrow next to the disk icon to select from your saved templates and edit / share as needed.

If you'd like to restrict a post to a specific Facebook List, Google+ Circle or other privacy options, you can! Start composing your post and choose the appropriate social network. Then click on the padlock icon to open the privacy selector where you can choose from your available options. For instance, if you have different circles set up within your Google+ Page, you can choose to share a post only with a specific circle.

This covers all of the basics you'll want to know to begin creating and scheduling posts. We will cover the different URL shorteners, parameters, and other advanced options later on.

In the next chapter, we're going really dig into sharing images via Hootsuite so that you'll be able to share great-looking images like a Pro.

How to Use Hootsuite to Share an Image

Statistics have shown that when posting updates and content to social networks, use of an image will improve your engagement significantly. That's partly due to the fact that 90% of information transmitted to the brain is visual, and visuals are processed 60,000x faster in the brain than text. In fact, according to Simply Measured, just one month after the introduction of Facebook Timeline for brands, visual content -- photos and videos -- saw a 65% increase in engagement.

However, the images that you use, and how you use them, matter. Make sure that you choose interesting images that viewers can connect to and be interested in. Furthermore, you should make sure that the images you use are large enough to fill the display space for each of the networks. Don't use tiny 100x100 thumbnails that look small even on smartphones.

A common technique is to include an image in your blog posts and then share those posts to Twitter, Facebook, LinkedIn and Google+. While that's a great way to share your new content, it may not be the most effective for a number of reasons. For starters, sharing a blog post to Twitter will not include an image - only the text of the title or whatever you choose to type into the tweet (unless you've set up Twitter Cards). And on Facebook and Google+, the images that are included may only be as thumbnails only.

There is a better way.

If you have Hootsuite Pro and have set up your social networks, you can easily share full images to Facebook and Google+, and even attach an image to your Twitter update! Here's how:

1. Open Hootsuite and start a new status update.
2. Copy the URL for your post and paste it into the link box and click Shrink. This will insert a shortened link into the status update.
3. Select one or more social networks. You will need to select at least one Twitter account. If you select a Facebook, Google+ or LinkedIn account, Hootsuite will generate a preview of your post.

4. Type in text for your Twitter update - you can copy and paste the blog Title from the preview, or type in something different.
5. Drag and drop an image into the status update field. This will add another shortened URL to the field and attach the image below for you to review.
6. You can choose to post the update immediately, or take advantage of Hootsuite's auto scheduling which will attempt to post your update at the optimum time.

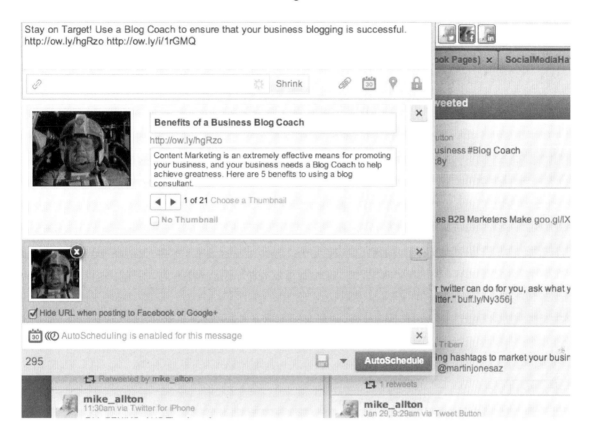

And that's it! You've now posted a full image to your Facebook and Google+ streams, and attached the image to a Twitter update. I regularly use this technique for new blog posts to ensure maximum engagement levels. Try it a few times and let us know how it goes for you!

A few additional notes:

First, while you must have a Twitter account selected to initially upload and attach an image, you can *then* feel free to deselect that Twitter account, and only share that post to Facebook or Google+.

Second, I have found that if I want to share an image post to Google+, it is best to do that as it's own post. If you include Facebook and Google+ together in the same shared image post, the Google+ share will revert to a link preview rather than an image. This is clearly a bug, and I will be one of the first to share the news when it is fixed.

Finally, you can feel free to include LinkedIn as a selected social network when sharing an image – the image just won't post. If you're sharing a link, it will be shared as you might expect as a standard link preview. So don't feel like you need to set up a separate post for LinkedIn if your text and link is otherwise the same.

Next, let's shift gears and talk about how you can use Hootsuite for one of the most interesting aspects unique to Twitter – Twitter Chats.

How to use Hootsuite to Manage Twitter Chats

One of the more interesting aspects of Twitter usage that has evolved over time is that of Twitter Chats. Chats on Twitter are conversations, often between complete strangers, that revolve around a specific hashtag. The hashtag is a requirement, as it is the linking of tweets through the hashtag that powers the chat. Instead of using Twitter.com or one of the available Twitter Chat tools, I recommend that you use Hootsuite.

Twitter Chat Explained

A Twitter Chat or Tweet Chat is using Twitter to talk about a common interest with others during a preset time. It's like an online chatroom where you add to the discussion by tweeting. Each time you tweet or respond to a tweet within the chat, you simply have to ensure that you include that chat's hashtag so that it's linked.

You can also start your own Twitter Chat. Simply pick a hashtag that isn't already used (just search the hashtag to see if anyone else is using it), and then promote it to your followers. Choose a time and topic and work on making sure that it won't be just you participating.

Why Chat?

First of all, let's just call this out. Participating in a Twitter Chat can be fun! It's exciting to suddenly be talking with people from all around the world on a topic, and have those tweets and comments come flying in.

But more importantly, from a business perspective, it's an opportunity for you to connect with and engage other Twitter users in a way that you would never be able to accomplish on your own. By participating in the conversation and injecting your comments, you create opportunities for you to connect with new people, whether they're influencers in your industry or potential clients.

Hootsuite Chatting

If you're already using Hootsuite, as I am, to manage and monitor your social network activity, this will be a natural extension of that usage. And note, since you can connect multiple Twitter accounts to Hootsuite, you can actually participate in a Twitter Chat using Hootsuite as yourself or your brand, or both!

What makes Hootsuite better than Twitter web is that you can save a chat as a stream in your Hootsuite dashboard. This will let you monitor the chat easily, as well as jump into it at any time without having to remember the right hashtag or do a search. And as we mentioned in our earlier chapter on Tabs & Streams, you can actually create a Tab just for Twitter Chats, and have multiple chat streams saved within it (up to 10).

Within Hootsuite, in the upper right corner, do a search for the hashtag of the chat you with to join. You'll see a number of tweets show up in the results. At the bottom of the results, there's a button to "Save as Stream." This will allow you to save that search, and that chat hashtag, as a stream in your tab.

Upgrade my plan

Quick Search

 ✕

 ▾ #TwitterSmarter

 S

MadalynSklar
4:07pm via Twitter for iPhone

@sdepolo @drjoyce_knudsen Thank you for sharing Stacey! We missed you on the #TwitterSmarter chat last week!

assistantbecky
3:59pm via Twitter Web Client

RT @MadalynSklar: The 7 Best SEO Twitter Chats You Should Be Utilizing buff.ly/2uypX1e #TwitterSmarter pic.twitter.com/bIGAZDsssA

bph
3:46pm via Twitter for Android

RT @MadalynSklar: The 7 Best SEO Twitter Chats You Should Be Utilizing buff.ly/2uypX1e #TwitterSmarter pic.twitter.com/bIGAZDsssA

rajastanirajpu1
3:39pm via Twitter for Android

RT @MadalynSklar: Be sure to join our

Save as Stream

You can now view the chat as it occurs in a saved stream. You can use the Hootsuite tools to favorite and reply to tweets from other participants, and use the Compose dialogue to create tweets of your own. Just be sure to always include the hashtag for the chat.

On a regular basis, the Hootsuite stream will check for and indicate that there are new tweets available to view. Remember that each stream has its own refresh button so you don't have to refresh your entire screen - just that chat stream.

The beauty of using Hootsuite is that it allows you to monitor and manage your total Twitter activity simultaneously. I mention this because, if you're involved in a chat and you're providing valuable information, other participants and observers are likely to ReTweet your tweets and mention you, and may even send you a direct message if they want to have a private conversation. Hootsuite allows you to easily manage all of these facets at the same time. If you like the idea of using a dedicated Tab for chats, you can always add a Mentions and Direct Message stream to that tab, alongside your saved chats.

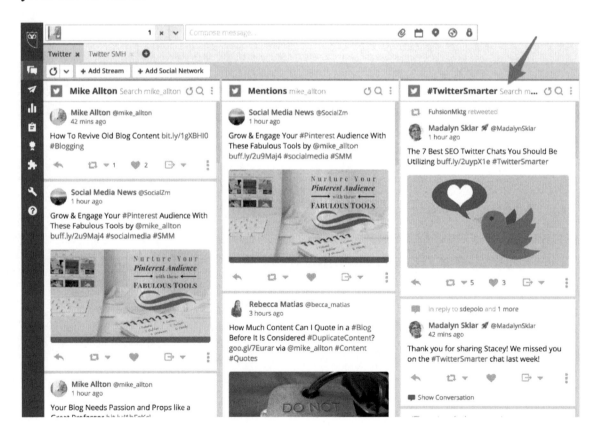

I would encourage you to find a couple of scheduled chats that are on topics that interest you, and take place at a convenient time for your schedule.

Next, we're going to cover how to automate your social media activity with Hootsuite (and why that can be good thing).

How to Use Hootsuite to Automate Social Media Activity

Automation Options

Within Hootsuite, you have a couple of ways in which you can automate some social media activity. First, you can schedule posts in advance, using the three available options we covered in the chapter on posting. Second, you can set up RSS feeds to be auto shared.

RSS/Atom

The RSS option within Hootsuite is a powerful one. With it, you can grab the RSS feed from any website, be it your own or someone else's, and set up Hootsuite to automatically check that feed on a regular basis and share one or more posts if there is new content. A Free Hootsuite account permits 2 RSS feeds, while a Pro account allows an unlimited number.

To add or manage your RSS feeds, click on the profile icon in the upper right corner from within the dashboard. Select **Account & Settings** and then **RSS/Atom** and you will see any feeds you've already set up. Tap the + button to add a new feed, and paste in the URL for the feed.

Each feed can only be connected to one network, so if you want to share to more than one network, you'll need to set up each one individually.

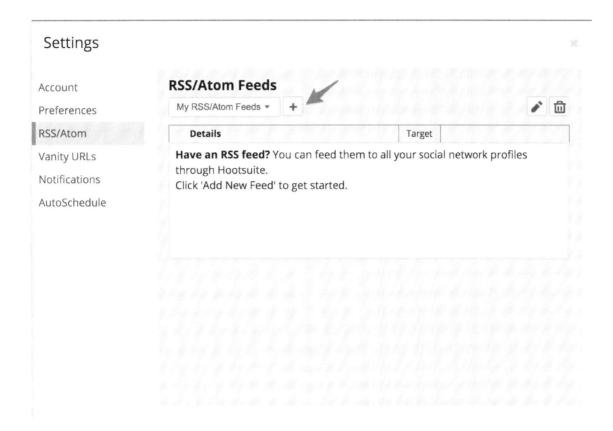

Once you select a network from the drop down box, you can select how often to check for new posts, and how many posts to share at a time, if there are any. Typically, you'll only want to share one post at a time, and check once a day, but depending on the source and your purpose, you may want to check more often or share more posts.

One option to consider is that Hootsuite will allow you to prepend the text of the post with whatever text you wish. The suggested usage is something like "New Post" but you can be creative. For instance, you might include the Twitter handle of the site's author so they get a mention every time you share.

Finally, you can select which URL shortener to use. Hootsuite offers four: ow.li, owl.ly, ht.li and ht.ly. LI and LY are country codes from Lichtenstein and Libya. All four shorteners include complete metrics, and the HT shorteners also include social sharing options. We will dig into the differences of each in a later chapter, but you're free to choose any one you want.

Once you've chosen your settings, click Save Feed and it will be added to your list.

When viewing your list of feeds, you can turn feeds on or off, and edit or delete feeds as needed.

Automation Uses & Cautions

So, first and foremost, let me be clear that I am **not** advocating that businesses put their social media on auto pilot. Simply using this RSS feature to automatically spam content to your social networks is not genuine and will do *nothing* to further your business goals.

Let me repeat that: **spamming posts to social media will not further business goals.**

However, there are certainly instances where automatically posting content can and should be considered.

Supplement Rich Content

The first instance where automation is great is when it's used as a supplement to the great content and posts you're already sharing. RSS feeds from trusted sources can be used to regularly share information with your followers that is helpful and interesting.

Be careful though. If all you do is share content from other sources, your followers won't need you! They can go straight to the source. Make sure that your sources are fantastic, and make an effort to add additional value through comments and your other shares.

Maintain Activity During Off Times

One of the keys to a successful social media presence is consistency. Businesses need to be consistently active on their social networks. But not every business owner has the time to post every day, and smaller businesses will really struggle during weekends, evenings, holidays and vacations. Scheduling posts and using an RSS feed for selective automated activity can help a business remain active, even when the business owner or social media manager is off.

Be careful though. Businesses who have scheduled or automated activity must be mindful of what they have scheduled, and be aware of any circumstances that may require a change in what's scheduled. A typical example is when a business has scheduled posts going out during a local or national crisis. It's possible that such posts may be considered inappropriate, so they'll need to be reviewed and perhaps postponed. If you want to "go quiet" with your business on social media, check the Publisher within Hootsuite to see any scheduled posts, and pause all RSS feeds.

Sharing Old Content

Businesses that are actively creating content and participating in social media are going to develop two things:

- an archive of old articles
- a growing follower base that missed older posts

Therefore, I think it's a good idea for businesses to regularly share their older articles. They will put those articles in front of new eyes, as well as offer businesses a way to share and introduce them that might be different than before. You can tweet a different title, or write a different commentary.

Be careful though. You don't want to share too many old posts, and you don't want to share old posts that are not longer valid or helpful. Marketers refer to content that continues to be interesting and educating as "evergreen" content. If you use the bulk scheduler within Hootsuite, you can maintain a spreadsheet of your evergreen content (I'll tell you how in a moment). Be mindful of your audience, not only what they're interested in, but what volume of posting they can tolerate.

Next, we're going to cover how to use Hootsuite to curate and share great content.

How to Use Hootsuite to Curate and Share Content

Social Streams

A good rule of thumb for businesses who want to present a well-rounded and effective social media presence is to maintain an 80/20 ratio for posted content. 80% of your social media posts should be from or about other people, while just 20% should be from or about you. If all you're doing is talking about yourself, fewer people will be interested. Therefore, finding and utilizing sources for great content to share and re-share is a real challenge. That's where Hootsuite can streamline the process.

First, make sure that on your key social networks (Twitter, Facebook, LinkedIn and Google+), you are carefully following and connecting with people who provide valuable content and information. If you're following random people just to get follow-backs and ramp up your follower count, you'll dilute the value of your home streams (not to mention have tons of followers who likely aren't genuinely interested in you).

Next, set up Streams within one or more Tabs and connect the news feeds from your social networks. For Facebook and LinkedIn, you will be able to see the latest updates from your connections. For Twitter and Google+, you can connect your Home stream as well as specific Lists or Circles you've set up.

As you continue to create new connections and curate great Lists and Circles of thought leaders and influencers, you can jump into this Tab and see a steady stream of fantastic updates and shared posts. Any time you see a great post, you can choose to share it right within Hootsuite.

But wait, there's more.

What makes Hootsuite particularly valuable for this purpose is that not only will have you have a single place to go to check out updates from all your networks, if you find an update on one network, you can share it to any of your other networks! If you've just hopped into Twitter, all you can do is

ReTweet to the account you're logged into. But when I call up my Technology News list within Hootsuite and see an interesting tweet from someone, I can send it to either my personal or my branded Twitter account, as well as any of my other social media accounts, and I can also choose to AutoSchedule it and space out my posts, rather than sharing a bunch of posts all at once.

Check your streams once or twice a day to look for great content from interesting people, and share it with your followers. Add in some of your own thoughts and information where appropriate, and use Hootsuite's AutoSchedule to space everything out.

Hootsuite Syndicator

The other method for finding outstanding content and news stories to share is by using the Hootsuite Syndicator, a feature released by Hootsuite in 2013. The Syndicator allows you to set up one or more RSS feeds from whatever websites and sources you're interested in. For instance, business advisors might subscribe to feeds from Forbes and Wall Street Journal and Business Insider.

Just like with the Social Streams, you can set up a new Tab or create one or more streams within an existing Tab. I like to have an RSS Tab with one or more streams within it to keep things organized. You can put all your RSS feeds into a single stream, or perhaps have different streams for different topics, or even one source per stream - whatever makes the most sense to you.

> *Time-saving Tip: Set up a stream with an RSS feed from your own site. This makes it easy for you to re-share versions of your latest blog post to Twitter, which you'll want to do at least a couple of times.*

Click on Add Stream, select the Apps tab, and click on Hootsuite Syndicator. That will add the RSS app to your account.

You'll have an empty stream and if you click on the RSS icon for that stream, you'll open the Hootsuite Subscription Manager.

Here you can add as many RSS feeds as you'd like. Once you have one or more subscriptions, they will appear in the list and you can delete or edit them as needed. You can also group them into categories, which is great if you have a number of different RSS feeds for different purposes.

If you've previously exported your Google Reader feeds into an .xml file, or perhaps run a quick export from Feedly or whatever other RSS reader you're using, you can upload your .xml file and import all of your feeds at once.

The other method for adding new subscriptions is even easier if you're using Google Chrome as your web browser. Simply install the Chrome Extension for Hootsuite, Hootlet, and now any time you click on an RSS feed icon or link, a small Hootsuite dialogue box will come up prompting you to subscribe to that feed [link to Chrome Store].

Once set up, all you have to do is check your RSS tab each morning and look for great articles to share. For instance, I often share really fabulous posts from Jeff Bullas, Heidi Cohen and Copyblogger. They publish articles daily that provide tremendous value to those interested in learning more about content marketing and social media. By sharing them, I not only help my own followers, but I add variety and interest to my social network streams.

Some articles I will share to multiple accounts, and others maybe just one or two, depending on the topic. For instance, informational articles, particularly on blogging and content marketing, I will usually share to all four of my branded accounts. Platform-specific articles, like something on Facebook Contests, I might only share to Facebook. And I usually reserve Tech news for one or both of my Twitter accounts.

When you see an article that you're interested in sharing, you can first click on the title and the text of the article will open in a pop-up window, giving you an opportunity to read or at least review the article and make sure it's worth sharing. You might also highlight a bit of the text that you can quote in your post. Close that window and then click on the left arrow icon to share the post using Hootsuite. This will grab the title of the post and the shortened link and populate the Compose dialogue box.

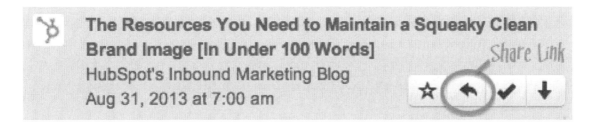

Now that you have an initial message ready, you can edit it as much as you want. Here's where you can paste in that quote and add some commentary of your own, as well as edit the Title and/or add some Hashtags to help link the post. Select one or more social networks and then send. Just like with the social shares above, I recommend using the AutoSchedule. AutoSchedule will ensure that your posts are shared at the optimum time for each network, as well as space out each of the posts so they're staggered.

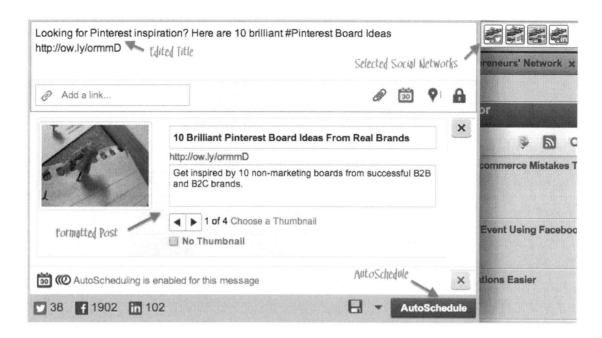

If you use the AutoSchedule, or manually schedule each post, you can take a few minutes in the morning to review the latest articles and share whichever ones seem most appropriate and interesting. You can then go about your day knowing that your social networks will be sharing interesting content throughout the day.

These are some of the ways businesses can use Hootsuite to maintain a consistent presence on social media that provides real value to your followers and potential customers.

In the next chapter, we'll get into how to use the HootLet Extension available for Hootsuite users.

How to Access Hootsuite via Web, Mobile, App or Extension

Hootsuite via Web

Accessing your Hootsuite account using any of the available web browsers on your computer is certainly the most common way to use Hootsuite. It gives you access to all of the available features, as well as easy access to your account, settings and the App Directory.

One of the reasons I use the web interface most often is that I can use multiple browsers to have multiple Hootsuite accounts open for myself and any clients for whom I am actively monitoring their social media activity. I've found Chrome to perform the best, though there are no major differences in functionality or appearance between browsers that I've noted.

[Web link]

Hootsuite via Mobile

Hootsuite does offer a mobile app. It is a dedicated and native app that is specifically available for iOS or Android, and not a mobile-version of their site. Hootsuite specifically does not use a mobile website so that you can always choose to access the full "desktop" version if needed from your mobile device.

The mobile app is designed to give you easy access to the most commonly needed features, namely monitoring and posting. As a result, it is somewhat limited. The mobile app supports multiple Twitter accounts, Facebook profiles and Pages, LinkedIn profiles and Foursquare. It does not support LinkedIn Company Pages, Groups or Google+.

"Tabs" are displayed in a series of groups, with Streams listed within each tab. Just as with the full version, you can add more tabs and multiple streams within tabs, and you're not limited to one network per tab. You can create search streams for multiple networks within a single tab, or combine multiple Twitter accounts, or whatever configuration works best for you.

[iOS link] [Android link]

Hootsuite via App

What many may not realize is that Hootsuite also offers a dedicated application that can be installed on your computer and run separately and independently of your browser window. It is essentially a stand-alone Chrome browser that is dedicated to Hootsuite. If you're only worried about your own Hootsuite account, this is probably not necessary, but if you manage more than one Hootsuite account, this offers you an additional logged in instance.

[Download link]

Hootsuite via Extension: Hootlet

One of the coolest options for Hootsuite users that I've reserved for last is the Extension: Hootlet. While limited only to Chrome and Firefox users, it's a particularly handy tool. Once installed, any time you're on a website or article, you can choose to click the Hootsuite icon in your toolbar to open a Hootsuite Compose box and share the post using Hootsuite, allowing you select your connected social networks and even AutoSchedule the post.

And Hootsuite has recently updated the Chrome Extension so that now, whenever you click a share button on an article for Twitter or Facebook, a new button appears on the share dialogue that you can use to open a Hootsuite Message dialogue box. The button looks like this:

What's great is that this takes a simple Facebook share button and adds the capability for you to use Hootsuite to share to multiple social networks, and even schedule the share for a later date and time. While you had that capability all the time thanks to the Hootlet, this button is a great reminder!

[Chrome extension] [Firefox extension]

BONUS: Hootbar

If you're using Firefox, you can add a new toolbar that brings even more ease and functionality to your browser. With the Hootbar, you can send a tweet with a link to whatever page you're on, as well as begin composing a tweet and then send it to the Hootlet for further customization and additional social networks.

[Download link]

These are the four (plus a bonus) ways businesses can access Hootsuite to maintain a consistent presence on social media that provides real value to your followers and potential customers.

Next, we'll get into how to Bulk Schedule posts using Hootsuite.

How to Bulk Schedule Messages

What is Hootsuite Bulk Scheduling?

Within Hootsuite, we have covered how you can use the Compose tool to create a message that gets sent out to one or more selected social networks. And we also covered how you can choose a specific date and time for the post to be published, or use Hootsuite's AutoSchedule to pick a time within the next 2 - 12 hours when it's more likely that your network's followers will be online. But what is this Bulk Schedule option that keeps coming up?

Bulk Schedule is when you set up multiple posts to be published, all at once. It's achieved by uploading a special spreadsheet, which we will dig into in a moment, and that tells Hootsuite the time and content of every post you want to schedule.

There is a maximum of 350 total scheduled messages across all of your networks for your Hootsuite account, and you can specify multiple social networks when uploading your spreadsheet.

However, if you're going to bulk schedule messages it's probably best that you have different spreadsheets with different times for different social networks, so keep that overall limit of 350 scheduled messages in mind.

What *can* you Bulk Schedule with Hootsuite?

With your trusty spreadsheet, you can set specific date and times and specify text and a link to share at that time. Links are automatically shortened using your default Hootsuite link shortener. Your total post, including both text and the link, is limited in characters by whichever network you're posting to. Since it's likely that you will be posting to Twitter, that means a limit of 140 characters. When you upload the spreadsheet, all posts in the sheet are scheduled for the selected networks, so you can create one spreadsheet for Twitter and a different one for Facebook where you a greater character allowance.

Links are optional, so you can share plain text messages whenever you wish.

What *can't* you Bulk Schedule with Hootsuite?

One drawback to Bulk Scheduling is that you cannot include images. Normally, if you have a Hootsuite Pro account, you can Compose a post, drop an image onto the post, and have that image posted as an image to Twitter or Facebook, rather than just a link preview. The uploaded spreadsheet for bulk scheduling offers no such option.

You may not bulk schedule duplicate messages, though you can use the same spreadsheet later on to reschedule posts if it makes sense to do so.

How to set up Hootsuite Bulk Scheduling

Bulk Scheduling obviously starts with the spreadsheet. Your Hootsuite dashboard will provide you with a template.

The spreadsheet has three columns: Date, Message, Link. You do not need to label the columns. Each row is a new scheduled post, so if you want to schedule 15 posts your spreadsheet should have 15 rows of information. As mentioned earlier, the Message and Link column text needs to be limited in characters for whatever networks you're posting to, but otherwise can say whatever you want.

The Date column data is what's tricky, as the date must be in a very specific format of mm/dd/yyyy hh:mm or dd/mm/yyyy hh:mm. You'll need to tell Excel that that data in column is Text and not to be changed or it will try to convert your dates into a different display that will fail your upload.

Post times must end in a 5 or 0, like 10:00 or 10:45. If you put an odd time into your spreadsheet Hootsuite will round up and then post. You also need to set all times to be at least ten minutes into the future so make sure you're giving yourself enough time to schedule the activity.

Save your spreadsheet as a CSV (comma separated values) and then upload it. Hootsuite will either accept it or tell you that there are errors to fix.

To upload, you can open a Compose box, click on the Schedule button and then click on the "bulk schedule posts" link. You can also go to the Publisher tab and click on the "Schedule in Bulk" button in the upper left.

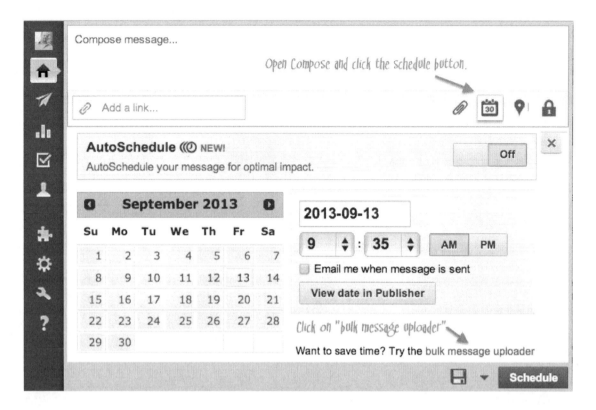

This will open the Bulk Scheduling dialogue box where you can upload your CSV file, select the format you chose to use for your post dates, and select one or more social networks.

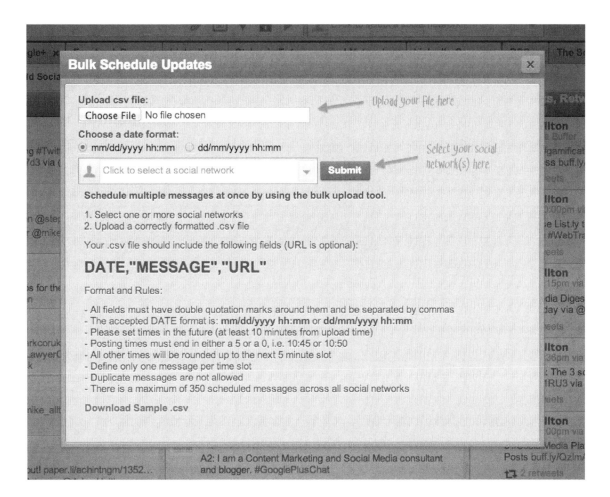

If there are any issues with your uploaded file, Hootsuite will tell you what the problems are and on which lines. For instance, if your posting to Twitter and you have a status update that is too long, Hootsuite will tell you that row #2 has too many characters for Twitter. At that point, no posts will be scheduled, just in case it's critical that the post(s) with an error be scheduled. You will need to correct or delete the status update(s) indicated, and then resubmit your CSV file.

This is, of course, the point where most users get frustrated, and where that website I referenced earlier can come in handy. You may run into a bunch of errors, particularly if you're uploading a lot of updates at once, and have trouble getting them all corrected. The first time you try the bulk scheduler, I recommend scheduling just a couple of posts so you can make sure that your spreadsheet format is correct, and you get the hang of the system.

And be patient. Take the time to craft valuable and meaningful updates, and take the time to assemble and correct your spreadsheet, and you may be richly rewarded with an incredible savings of time in the long run.

Now that you have the basic technique and tools to set up bulk scheduling, let's look at some of the viable ways businesses might use this Hootsuite feature.

Uses for Hootsuite Bulk Scheduling

If you don't have a Buffer account, you can use Hootsuite bulk scheduling to craft and share messages and activity using your old content. Make sure, of course, that the article information is still valid and appropriate. I do prefer and use Buffer for this purpose.

Another easy use case for bulk scheduling is when you or your social media manager are going to be out of the office, say for a week's vacation, you can bulk schedule daily posts and updates to ensure that specific messages are being shared throughout the week. If you were going to do this, I would still encourage you or a representative to continue to monitor your social networks so that you can respond to comments and feedback in a timely manner.

Businesses who are active in content marketing, social media marketing and content curation often actually forget to simply mention themselves ands what they do. Is certainly OK to talk about yourself now and then on social networks and remind people who you are and what you do. Bulk Schedule is a great way to do this because you can decide in advance what you're going to say, how often you're going to say it, and then schedule it. This ensures regular communication but keeps it in line and in proportion to everything else that you're saying.

By the same token, if your business is regularly going to be closed or unavailable due to holidays, conferences or other circumstances, you can pre-schedule appropriate messages so your followers and customers know what to expect. You can create an Out of Office spreadsheet with all of the year's holidays and special dates by row, and a custom message for each.

Speaking of holidays, how about having some fun and wishing everyone a Happy Boxing Day or Happy Groundhog Day! You could set up reminders for yourself of course, or just have another spreadsheet that you load up and update each January with the coming year's dates and messages.

Do you find yourself regularly sharing the same messages or reminders? Perhaps you're hosting or attending a weekly Twitter chat, or maybe at the end of every month it's helpful for you to remind your followers and customers to send in their information or files. Plug that into a Bulk Schedule so that you can be assured that it will go every time you need it to, leaving you free to concentrate on more important things.

As you can see, there are a LOT of uses for Bulk Scheduling social media posts. What you aren't seeing in this list are replacements for normal, day-to-day activity. Social media activity needs to be genuine and meaningful. But when we're simply communicating information, like our hours on Christmas Eve, it's almost better to schedule that well in advance and know that it's taken care of.

One final word on scheduling: always be mindful of what you have scheduled to post at any given time. You can open your Hootsuite Dashboard and click on Publisher to see what's scheduled to go out. If something happens and it would suddenly be inappropriate to be sharing the messages you have scheduled, make sure you log in and reschedule or delete them.

Now that you know everything there is to know about posting updates and scheduling them, it's time we went over how to use Hootsuite for Social Listening.

How to Use Hootsuite for Social Listening

What is Social Listening?

Of course, it helps if we're all on the same page as to what Social Listening means. The details will vary from business to business and industry to industry, but the core principle is that brands will listen to conversations taking place on social media and look for opportunities to participate and engage customers and prospects.

First, a business will identify specific words and phrases that might be part of a conversation that would apply to the business. For instance, if your business solves specific problems, you would listen for people talking about those kinds of issues. You might find opportunities to provide assistance or resources, or to reach out to individuals in need.

Second, a business will identify key influencers. These are people who may be well-known in the industry, or perhaps in roles where a referral could go a long way. For instance, gaining the interest and support of someone more established on Twitter, where they may have a much larger following, might result in getting a ReTweet or mention that helps extend the reach and visibility of your business tremendously.

Conversational Listening with Hootsuite

To begin listening for key conversations, follow these steps:

1. Identify specific terms to listen for. Do some test searches and refine the terms as needed in order to achieve the kinds of results you're looking for.

2. Create a new Stream for each Term or Phrase. I recommend having a specific Tab set up for Conversations and then you can have up to ten streams within that Tab. Each stream can be a specific term or phrase, and can be set up to search Twitter or Google+ (you can search Facebook and LinkedIn as well, but only conversations from your existing connections, whereas the other platforms will search all Public posts).

- You can use the Quick Search in the upper right corner of your Hootsuite Dashboard to look for terms and phrases that might work for you. Once you find one, click on the Save as Stream button and it will be added as a stream within your existing tab.

- You can click on the Add Stream button and select a network, then select Search, and type in the phrase you want to search on.

3. Check your Conversations tab at least once a day to see what status updates have been posted that match those search terms, and respond if appropriate.

I have mentioned earlier that you can have canned responses set up as templates. Simply open the Compose box, type in your message, and click on the disk icon to save it as a template. You can then call up that message whenever needed. This is particularly useful when social listening, as you will often be providing the same basic answer and resources. Just make sure to edit your message before sending to customize it for the specific situation and individual.

You can also send tweets or updates that you find in your search to other Team members. We're going to get into Teams in more detail in another article, but the idea here is that larger businesses may have multiple people involved, and certain people may be better suited to respond to specific inquiries. An example I've given before is that of a law office, where an office manager may be responsible for all initial social media monitoring and listening, but any serious enquiries or opportunities would be forwarded to one of the attorneys in the office for a more professional response.

If your business is restricted to a specific geographic area, say, only the Greater St. Louis Area, then you have the option of geo-locating your search results and only seeing messages posted by people within your area. This will obviously filter out updates from people whom you're not interested in targeting as a potential customer.

Yet another reason for using Conversational Listening is for Customer Service. You can set up search streams for an instance of where people are talking about you and your company, either directly or indirectly, and engage those customers in whatever way is appropriate. A simple is example would be if someone decided to complain about your brand on Twitter.

Unless they happened to mention your Twitter handle, you'd have no idea that they said anything about you. If you're listening though, you can at least give yourself an opportunity to respond and try to make the situation better.

Brands can also use listening as a means to monitor competitors. By setting up search streams, lists and circles, you can keep an eye on what your competition is doing and make sure that you're positioned to respond to any sudden sales or other developments which might affect your own business or customers.

Keep in mind that you can have up to 50 tabs set up within your Hootsuite Dashboard, and each tab can have up to 10 streams saved, so you can create whatever tab and stream combinations you need. Every time you log into your Hootsuite account and select one of these tabs, all of the saved streams will update. And you can add or delete streams whenever needed, so don't be shy about creating temporary streams that you might only use for a week or even a day, then delete later. When I'm doing any kind of research into social media activity and conversations, I will save the streams so I can keep referring back to them for as long as I need them. You can do the same thing when researching customers, discussion topics, other brands and so on.

Influencer Listening with Hootsuite

As we mentioned earlier, it's important for every business to begin to identify key influencers and thought leaders in their industry. By doing so, you:

1. Follow them and gain insight into your own business and industry as a result of reading what they say and share.

2. Create opportunities for you to share and ReTweet these key thoughts and links to your own followers, creating value.

3. By sharing and ReTweeting, and actively participating in the online conversations happening around these updates and individuals, you begin to link yourself with those individuals.

4. The more you engage with and show an interest in these influencers, the more interest they will show in you. But it has to be genuine. ReTweeting

me 25 times a day is not going to get me to show interest in you and your business.

Now, there are different kinds of influencers, so you should have specific profiles and goals in mind. Are you looking for leaders in your industry who might help build your reputation through association? Or perhaps you're looking for key C-level executives who can help you land critical accounts, or perhaps someone else.

Finding these influencers is achieved a couple of different ways. You can do a quick search and change to Twitter Users. Type in names or keywords or businesses or whatever makes sense for the kind of person you're looking for, and see what comes up. Within the list of Twitter users, you can click on any name and their profile will pop up and you can decide whether or not you want to follow that person.
Or, alternatively, you can search on topics and look for people talking about and demonstrating expertise and influence in specific areas.

Rebekah Radice (RebekahRadice)

100,602	36,806	88,069
Followers	Following	Updates

Location Los Angeles, CA

Bio Entrepreneur, Author, Founder, CMO https://t.co/N2AjUXrHde, marketing/training firm for growth leaders. Speaker. Creator Authority Matrix. Success Multiplier.

Twitter http://twitter.com/RebekahRadice

Website https://t.co/8yhM89JNyp

| Follow | Unfollow | DM | Reply | Add To List |

When looking at someone's Twitter bio within Hootsuite, you can see how many followers they have, how many updates they've posted, their location and their Bio text. You can also select a Timeline tab to see their latest tweets.

Once you've identified someone, following them is just the first step. You should then begin to form a relationship with that individual, and spend an appropriate amount of time compared to what you hope to get out of the relationship.

You may want to add that person to a new or existing Twitter List to help keep tabs on the profile, and can do so using the Add to List button at the bottom of the bio box.

You can send them a Direct Message if you think it would be appropriate, but generally I advise starting by making it a point to regularly ReTweet, favorite and reply to the tweets they're sending on a daily basis. Begin to start conversations with these individuals, and make intelligent comments. Ask good questions and offer genuine, thoughtful compliments, and you will begin to make an impression. At an appropriate time, Make The Ask - whatever it is you are hoping they will do for you, whether it's to make an introduction, ReTweet one of your tweets, or something else.

By laying the groundwork of ReTweeting, favoriting and other comments, you've created value for the influencer. That way, when you ask them to do something for you, they'll feel like they're reciprocating, and not just doing you a favor.

Mobile Listening

With the Hootsuite app, you can set up and save Twitter searches and streams similar to the Desktop dashboard.

You can add a new stream and set up the search, or, even easier, start a new search and if you like it save it as a stream.

CONVERSATIONS

 setting up HootSuite
Search

 social media help geoco...
Search

 Streams   Search   Stats   Contacts   Settings

These are the ways businesses can use Hootsuite to listen to the conversations taking place on social media, whether about the brand or the industry, and look for opportunities to connect with and engage customers and potential customers.

Next, we'll get into how to set up and use Hootsuite Teams.

How to Set Up and Use Hootsuite Teams

What are Hootsuite Teams?

Hootsuite allows businesses to create a hierarchy of structure and functionality within the dashboard in order to facilitate internal communication and workflow. Hootsuite's Team structure is comprised of Organization, Teams, Team Members and Social Profiles.

Organization: this is the highest level entity in Hootsuite and would typically represent your entire business and account. An Organization contains Teams, Team Members and Social Profiles.

Teams: these are groups of users collaborating together on various Social Profiles within an Organization.

Team Members: these are users invited to manage Social Profiles within a Team.

Hootsuite account administrators can completely tailor their organization by creating and customizing Teams, shuffling and assigning Team Members, and adding and arranging Social Profiles to best suit your needs.

With this structure in place, administrators can manage a variety of Teams and permission sets. The permission levels are very granular, but default permissions can be set and applied to each new Team Member as they are created.

New Teams can be created on the fly, and multiple Teams can be merged if needed.

How to Create Hootsuite Teams

To get started, you first have to have one or more Organizations. Go to your Profile within the Hootsuite Dashboard and click on Start Collaborating. This will get you started on creating your first Organization. You can specify a name for the organization (typically your business), and you can select all possible Social Profiles that are associated with that Organization.

Once finished, you'll see your Organization control center that displays all of your Teams, Team Members and Social Profiles. Initially, it will be just you, and you'll have no Teams. You can add more Team Members by clicking on the Invite Members tab and inserting their email addresses. If you have Teams already set up, you can assign them to appropriate Teams immediately.

To begin creating Teams, simply drag one or more Team Members into the Teams area, or click on Add a Team. Similar to your Organization, you will be prompted to create a Team name, and to assign relevant Social Profiles. Again, this is where Team functionality is so appropriate, as your Marketing Team may not need access to the same social networks and accounts as your Customer Service Team.

Once you have your first Organization, Team, Team Member and Social Profiles set up, your dashboard will begin to look something like this:

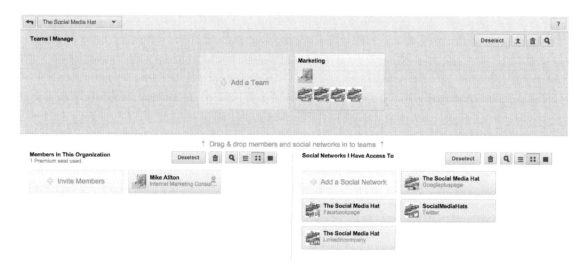

You can create multiple Organizations and switch back and forth as needed using the selector in the upper left corner. Within each Organization, you can add and edit your Teams, Team Members and Social Profiles easily. Each Team, Team Member and Social Profile has a settings icon in the upper left corner if you mouse over that entity that gives you access to manage assignments and permissions.

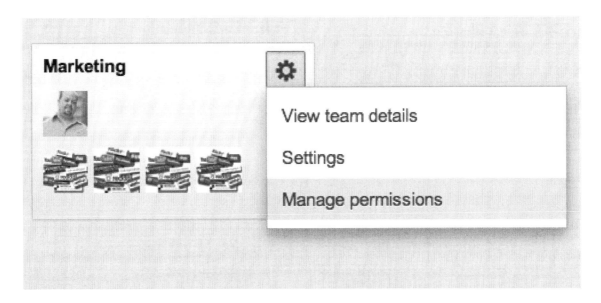

Hootsuite Message Assignment

As mentioned, if one Team Member sees a tweet or status update that another Team or Team Member needs to see and respond to, they can Assign that Message to whomever it would be appropriate. This initiates an internal workflow where the initial message, assignment and resolution is all documented, and your Hootsuite administrator view and monitor assignments as needed.

Hootsuite Conversations

Hootsuite includes an internal chat system for Teams and Team Members that they can use to communicate with each other without having to leave the Hootsuite dashboard. While great for team communication, particularly for remote teams, the real value is in it's integration with the rest of Hootsuite.

Team Members can send any tweet or message from any connected social network into a Conversation. Teams can then discuss the message, like or ReTweet or even broadcast back out to social networks.

Using Conversations, Teams can discuss issues or opportunities that come up on social media, come up with a plan of action and response, and then implement it. With the breakneck pace at which social network communication flies, being able to quickly identify, collaborate and respond to such messages can be critical.

When teams of people are involved in communicating your brand and responding to customer needs and issues, it's important to have the option to discuss response strategies and communicate approved messaging.

For instance, suppose that a customer makes your team aware of an issue with your online ordering system. You can immediately communicate that message to your technical team, and initiate an internal discussion with customer support and ownership on how to publicly respond and communicate the issue. Once decided, team members can respond to the original customer, as well as push out approved and crafted messages to all branded and personal social channels.

Conversation windows can also pop out of the dashboard so you can monitor the conversation while working on other tasks.

Free versus Pro

Teams are a feature that is only found within the Hootsuite Pro and Enterprise editions. If you're an individual blogger or sole proprietor, or even a small business, Teams are not likely a required feature. Larger businesses, corporations and organizations though should already be using or considering a Pro account, and therefore have access to set up Teams.

Your Hootsuite Pro account includes 1 Team Member and up to 9 more can be added. Each additional Team Member is $9.00 a month. The plan also includes up to 50 social profiles. If you need more users and/or profiles, Hootsuite Enterprise is a great option.

Examples and Uses

Businesses who have a Marketing Department and a Customer Service Department might share the same Facebook Page with both department Teams, but have a separate Twitter account just for "help". Whenever the Marketing Department monitors a customer service issue where the client mentioned the primary Twitter account, the tweet can be forwarded to the Customer Service Team and they can respond and assist using their Twitter account.

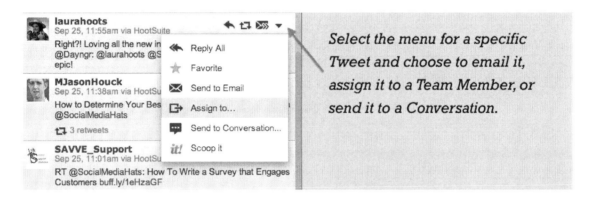

Select the menu for a specific Tweet and choose to email it, assign it to a Team Member, or send it to a Conversation.

Corporations who have a CEO and other C-level individuals and plan to use Hootsuite for managing their personal social networks can isolate those networks to an Executive Team and leave the branded accounts for the Marketing Team.

Companies can use a Business Development Team that is assigned sales leads that come in as comments and responses to social network status updates, and the Team can be given access to the networks and profiles most appropriate for lead generation and business development. For instance, such a Team may need access to LinkedIn profiles, company pages and groups, but not a branded Facebook Page.

Agencies and Individuals who want to use a single Hootsuite account to manage multiple businesses and brands can use Teams to represent each different brand, and connect and assign that brand's profiles accordingly. Though my personal preference is to set up a new Hootsuite account for each business that way have complete ownership and control over the Hootsuite profile.

Next, we'll get into how to set up and use Hootsuite's URL Shorteners.

How to Use Hootsuite
Shortened Links and Parameters

What's a Shortened Link?

Initially, shortened links were simply a means to take a long URL and shrink it into a link that still worked, yet used fewer characters, saving valuable space to be used in Tweets. Instead of a link like http://www.thesocialmediahat.com/... you would instead use something like http://WP.ly/wrgbergb which is a savings of 20+ characters.

To get a shortened link, you would simply plug your full URL into a link shortening service or tool and the tool would provide the shortened link.

Then, once you have your link in place, since the tool has to keep that shortened link active indefinitely anyways, the providers began offering analytics for links created. While any website can see how much traffic a specific page or blog post gets, and even where that traffic is coming from, a shortened link with analytics suddenly offers you the option of seeing traffic and interest from a specific link share. This opens up an immense number of campaign options and far more granular metrics.

Shortened URLs use a set domain followed by a unique combination of characters. Most link shortening services use one of the available international TLD (Top Level Domains) like .ly (Libya). Bit.ly is a very common example. Hootsuite uses four options: ow.ly and ht.ly, owl.li and htl.li. We'll get into the differences between those options in a moment. Li is for Liechtenstein.

Since Hootsuite metrics are dependent on the use of a Hootsuite shortened link, and since it is best practice to use shortened links in your social media shares anyways, I recommend always using a Hootsuite or custom shortened link.

Understanding Hootsuite URL Shorteners

So Hootsuite has these four options. What do they mean? What's the difference?

First, Libya, like many other countries, decided years ago to allow businesses and individuals to purchase domain names with their suffix. Every country in the world has a two character TLD suffix that is initially reserved for government use (.us or .uk for example), but each government is given the choice to sell domains using their assigned suffix. One of the most popular examples is Tuvalu who made .tv available to the world.

Libya's .ly ccTLD (country code Top Level Domain) is managed by the registry LYNIC and is primarily available to the people and businesses of Libya, but accepts applications from international entities. Domain names are registered at a premium cost of $75/year. Therefore, there are some who have concerns about how the use of such domains results in tacit support for the government of Libya. There have also been concerns about potential disruptions of service resulting in broken links.

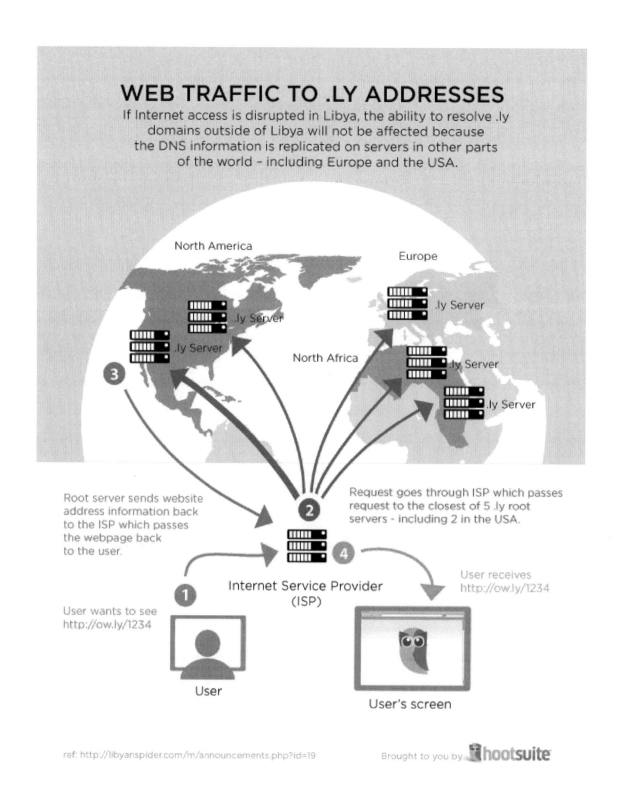

WEB TRAFFIC TO .LY ADDRESSES

If Internet access is disrupted in Libya, the ability to resolve .ly domains outside of Libya will not be affected because the DNS information is replicated on servers in other parts of the world – including Europe and the USA.

North America

Europe

.ly Server

.ly Server

.ly Server

North Africa

.ly Server

3

.ly Server

Root server sends website address information back to the ISP which passes the webpage back to the user.

Request goes through ISP which passes request to the closest of 5 .ly root servers - including 2 in the USA.

2

4

User receives
http://ow.ly/1234

Internet Service Provider
(ISP)

1

User wants to see
http://ow.ly/1234

User

User's screen

Therefore, Hootsuite purchased and implemented the owl.li shortener, which works exactly like ow.ly - just a different suffix.

The other interesting option that Hootsuite offers is ht.ly and htl.li. HTL is short for HootLet which is Hootsuite's extension and sharing tool. When these shorteners are used, users continue to gain the analytics benefits of ow.ly or owl.li, but also add the Social Sharing Bar at the top of resulting pages.

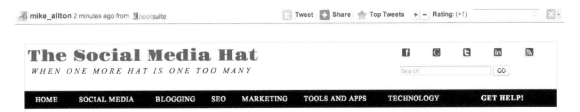

Once someone clicks through your link, the Hootsuite Social Sharing Bar will appear at the top of the site, encouraging them to rate and re-share the content. This is highly recommended for marketers and publishers!

Using Hootsuite URL Shorteners

By default, your Hootsuite dashboard and compose box will use ow.ly. To change your default link shortener, open the Compose box and click on the link field. That will reveal the link settings icon (a gear) that you can click to open Advanced Settings.

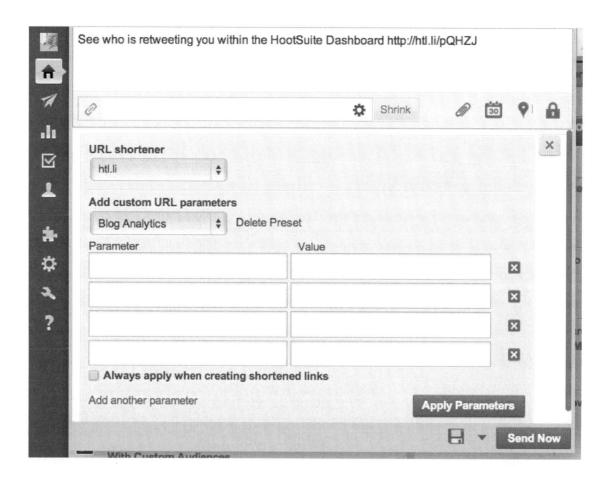

Most of the settings revolve around link parameters which we will explain and dig into in a moment, but the first option is a drop down where you can simply change which shortener you want to use for that post and all future posts. You can change this at any time.

Once you create a shortened link and share it, you can plug it into Hootsuite report: URL Click Stats to see activity for that specific link, regardless of where or when or how it was shared.

Setting up a Custom Link Shortener

Aside from the aforementioned choices, Hootsuite offers custom/vanity URL shortening services. Using a unique domain is a great way to increase brand awareness while still utilizing powerful analytics.

Pro users can choose to purchase this option in Settings > Preferences > URL and following the instructions. Enterprise customers should contact their Account Executive or complete the form at: Hootsuite.com/enterprise.

Link Parameters

What link parameters allow you to do is track analytics for specific URLs sent to your social media profiles. You can get a more fine-grained look at which social networks did or did not drive traffic to not just your site, but a specific blog post or landing page. It's the kind of setting that's great for A/B testing and campaign monitoring.

Start by opening the Compose box, insert the link you want to share, and click on the gear icon to open the advanced settings just like we did above.

Hootsuite allows you have preset parameters that can be applied on the fly to any link, or assigned to all links by default. "Google Analytics" is also set up as a default preset, which you can customize or add more as needed.

Within each preset, you can set a number of parameters (all options are listed below).

Choose a meaningful Campaign Name because you will be able to see it in both Hootsuite analytics and Google Analytics if you've connected your Google Analytics account to your Hootsuite account.

For Campaign Source, you may typically select a specific social network, like Twitter or Facebook.

For Campaign Medium, you can specify a social media account, if you or your client has, for instance, multiple Twitter accounts, or you might specify the kind of content being shared, like Blog Post.

This chart shows when and why URL parameters are used.

Campaign content (utm_content)	• For content-targeted ads and A/B testing. • Use to distinguish between ads or links that direct to the same URL.
Campaign medium (utm_medium)	• Required. • Use to identify a medium such as email or cost-per-click.

Campaign name (utm_campaign)	• For keyword analysis. • Use to identify a specific campaign or promotion.
Campaign source (utm_source)	• Required. • Use to identify a search engine, newsletter name or other source.
Campaign term (utm_term)	• For paid searches. • Use to mark keywords.

You can add parameters for Terms as well as Content when you have different ads that result in the same landing page (A/B testing).

Advanced social media marketing campaigns require advanced metrics in order to determine success and ROI. Implementing this level of sharing ensures that when you use Hootsuite analytics or Google Analytics, you'll be able to identify not just traffic via social, but also how specific campaigns performed.

How to Manage Your Google+ Brand Using Hootsuite

This chapter originally appeared on PlusYourBusiness.com, and has been updated and expanded. I am including a chapter specifically about Google+ because while Hootsuite may have been initially developed for Twitter and Facebook, it is actually extremely well-suited for Google+ Page Management.

When it comes to managing a Google+ Brand Page, my tool of choice is Hootsuite. The fact is, there's only so much you can do within the Google+ Dashboard itself. You can certainly craft a post and respond to notifications and comments, and view statistics. But you can't schedule activity, and you can't save searches and you can't source content for sharing.

With Hootsuite, I can connect one or more Brand Pages and do all of those things, and more! We're going to go through everything that you can do with Hootsuite to make your Google+ Page an active and vibrant community for your brand followers and connections.

Sharing Great Content

The first purpose that most people think of when they think about Hootsuite is using it to share posts to social networks, and without a doubt, that's the most common usage of the tool. And Hootsuite does have full support for Google+ Pages (not personal profiles), and even multiple Pages and Google+ Local Pages.

If you haven't already connected your Google+ account and set up one or more Pages, log into your Hootsuite Dashboard and click on the button with your name in the upper left corner to view your Organizations and Social Profiles. Click on Add a Social Network to open the add network dialogue box. Select Google+, authenticate your account, and you will be presented with a list of any Pages you are the manager of. Select any you wish to connect and then click Finished Importing. You'll now see that profile's pic in your list of available social profiles, with a small Google+ overlay image so you'll know which platform it's for.

You can now open the Compose dialogue box and craft social media messages like you normally would, and include your Google+ Page. We'll talk about Styling and Scheduling posts in a moment, but all of the Hootsuite basic principles and techniques apply here. You can shorten links, select up to 5 social profiles, pull in templated messages to share or create a post from scratch. And you can use the Hootlet Chrome Extension (which I love) to easily share any webpage or article you stumble across to your Google+ Page.

Note that the Hootlet is a fantastic option in this instance, even if the article itself has a Google+ sharing widget, since the widgets don't give you the option of sharing to a brand Page. If you find something you want to share with your business audience, using the Hootlet will save you from having to copy and paste URLs into Page status update boxes, and you get the full benefit of Hootsuite shortened links, scheduling and more.

But for me, what I really enjoy is using the Hootsuite Syndicator to bring in RSS feeds from my favorite blogs and news sources. I have a tab set up called RSS that I can click on at any time within my Hootsuite Dashboard. Once it refreshes, I'll see the latest articles from a dozen or more sites that I've curated, and with one click, I can begin crafting a post for my Google+ Page.

This saves me a tremendous amount of time, both for myself and for my clients who want to share interesting articles, industry news, and other viewpoints on a specific topic or topics.

Regardless of how you've found a post that you want to share, the next step is to decide what else you're going to say, and how you want it to look on Google+.

Styling

One of the great features that differentiates Google+ from other platforms is the ability to style and format posts. You can choose to share a link preview or an image, and within your text you can insert paragraph breaks, shortened links, and even make text bold and italic.

And the good news is that Hootsuite **fully supports** this level of formatting! That post was crafted entirely within Hootsuite.
There are a few caveats.

First, start by composing your post like you normally would within the Hootsuite dashboard. And just as though you were on Google+ itself, hit Enter for paragraph breaks and use the * and _ for basic formatting. (For more specific suggestions on formatting Google+ posts for maximum impact, read more here.)

If you want to share an image, you'll need to select at least one Twitter account to share the post to. Don't worry, you can unselect it later - that's just one of the quirks of Hootsuite. Once you have a Twitter account selected and your Google+ Page, drag your image into the Compose dialogue box. Hootsuite will upload it and add a shortened link for the image. Note that there's a checkbox now under your Compose field asking whether or not you want include that link when sharing to Facebook or Google+, and I would generally leave that checked. That will share the full image, and omit the link to the image from the description.

Sharing Images to Google+ or any social profile does require Hootsuite Pro.

Hashtags will also work perfectly, including having your first three displayed in the upper right corner of the post.

Mentions, unfortunately, do not yet work, so bear that in mind. You *can* edit a post later to include a mention link to someone's profile, but bear in mind that mentioning someone on a post that has already gone live will not result in a notification for that person. This is because your Google+ name doesn't have to be unique, so when you start to +Mention someone, a list of possible matches comes up. If you're on a third-party platform like Hootsuite, there's no such list.

However, those interested in making a great impression with influencers *do* have a workaround. Google+ posts can always take the ID number of a user's account and automatically convert that into a mention! (refer to the Appendix for more detailed instructions on obtaining a Google+ User ID)

And one final note: when crafting a post like this, it should only be used for

Google+ Pages. While you can share an image to both Google+ Pages and Facebook Pages and even Tweets, Twitter and Facebook will limit how much text you can include, and the styling of text to make it bold or italic is not supported on other networks. This technique is best used only for Google+ Pages, particularly if you want to schedule the post to be shared later. I have also noted on occasion that the Google+ share will end up only displaying a shortened URL instead of the image or link preview, so avoid combining Google+ with other platforms when sharing.

Scheduling

Which brings us to the next benefit of using Hootsuite for Google+ Page Management: Scheduling. Within Hootsuite, you have a number of options when it comes to sharing a post:

1. Share Now
2. AutoSchedule
3. Schedule
4. Bulk Schedule

Share Now is a great option when you have content within Hootsuite already that you want to share (like from RSS feeds discussed a moment ago), or are using the Hootsuite Hootlet, and don't want to take the time to open and log into your Google+ Page or Pages.

AutoSchedule is one of my favorite little tools within Hootsuite. At any time, if you want to share something using Hootsuite but do not want or need it to go out right away, clicking AutoSchedule will allow Hootsuite to automatically choose a time to share that post, typically within the next few hours, when Hootsuite thinks it will be most likely to be seen. If you know you want something to go out today or tomorrow at the latest, but have no other specific requirements, this is the option to choose. Not only will it stagger posts to your Google+ Page, it will ask stagger among any other social networks you're sharing to, so if you have a post you want to share to a few profiles they all won't go out at exactly the same time.

Once a post has been AutoScheduled, you can click on the Publisher screen, view the scheduled activity, and edit them if needed.

Schedule is your option to choose a specific date and time for your post. For businesses running a Google+ Page, this is a great option for Holiday messages, timed announcements, and messages that need to be communicated on a weekly basis (like specials, etc.). Schedule is also the option to use if you want to set up several days worth of posts, as AutoSchedule may only put an hour or two between them.

Bulk Schedule is an interesting option where you can upload a spreadsheet full of messages and links and specific time and dates for each message. While Bulk Schedule would support formatting and hashtags, it would not support sharing images (only links with link previews), so it's generally not the ideal tool for creating social activity on Google+. It is, however, a great option for businesses that want to share preset messages, like holiday hours. You could create your spreadsheet on January 1, upload it, and have your holiday greetings and messages scheduled for the entire year in advance.

Whichever method you choose should be based on when you think your audience and your message will be most likely to connect. For some that may mean during "peak usage" times, while for others you may want to avoid peak usage times and catch your audience when there's less competition for their attention. As well as being mindful of time zones and geographic differences. And then continue to test and measure and revise so that over time, you'll learn which methods and time and approaches work the best for your business and achieve the results you're looking for.

Social Listening

Posting and schedule posts to Google+ Pages is great, but that's only the beginning of a successful social media strategy. To truly be effective, brands and businesses must be *listening* to what's being said on Google+, and Hootsuite is great for that. The typical reasons for listening include Prospecting, Brand Monitoring and Customer Service, but the following technique can be used for all manner of purposes.

From within any Tab (typically a tab dedicated to your Google+ presence or specifically for monitoring), click on Add Stream and select the Search tab. Make sure that your Google+ Page is selected and then type in whatever search term(s) you want. You can search for your brand name or specific products to monitor when people are having conversations around your business, or you can put in more topical keywords to keep an eye out for people to follow or discussions to join.

You can have up to 10 streams saved within a tab at a time, so feel free to create several streams and see which ones bear the most fruit. The technique itself is easy - the art is in determining how you want to use it and the most appropriate keywords to be searching for.

At any time, you can share a specific post that appears within a stream, or even an entire stream, with your other Hootsuite Team Members.

You can leave comments on Google+ posts from within Hootsuite.

While you cannot +1 or Share posts yet, you *can* click on the timestamp for a specific post and open it within a new tab and then take additional actions from there.

But if *other* people have already +1'd or commented on a post, you can see the numbers for that post at the bottom of the post and click on them to see that post's activity.

Circle Monitoring

Finally, one of the really cool aspects of Google+ Page monitoring within Hootsuite is that as you set up circles of people on Google+, you can create streams within Hootsuite for any of those circles.

Adding such a stream works the same as adding any other new stream: click on Add Stream, make sure your Google+ Page is selected, choose Circles and then select whichever one you want.

Businesses who are taking full advantage of the power of Google+ Circles can do *so much* with this!

 - Businesses can follow their clients and listen to what they're talking about, watching for opportunities to help and support them.
 - Businesses can follow vendors and industry news Pages and pay attention to the latest developments in their niche.
 - Businesses can follow influencers in their industry and cull relationships

by participating in discussions and sharing updates.
 - Businesses can follow competitors.
 - Businesses can follow people who have engaged with them in the past and continue to grow those relationships.
 - Businesses can follow other Pages and People within the Team and help cross-promote activity.

So make sure that you're getting the most out of both your Google+ Page and your Hootsuite Dashboard by connecting them and following some of these best practices.

 - Share Great Content
 - Format Posts for Optimum Engagement
 - Schedule Posts to Reach a Larger Audience
 - Listen to What's Being Said
 - Monitor and Engage with Circles

If you have more questions about Google+ or Hootsuite, or are looking for more help managing your online community, let us know.

How to Hone Your Skills Using Hootsuite University

If you're interested in not only improving your mastery of Hootsuite, but of Social Media in general, Hootsuite's University is a great place to head next.

Who Should Consider Hootsuite University?

Social Media Managers

First, anyone who is charge of managing social media for a business should strongly consider going through a series of courses, and Hootsuite's is a great option. Social Media Managers may include dedicated company employees, or outside contractors like myself that a business may bring in as-needed or on a monthly retainer basis.

Hootsuite Consultants

Anyone interested in being a Hootsuite Partner and helping other businesses to set up and use Hootsuite needs to go through these courses. While Hootsuite doesn't require it, I think having this knowledge and the certification of being a Hootsuite Professional should be a requirement for any business considering hiring someone to help them with Hootsuite. And the reason is simple: there's more to using Hootsuite than just connecting some social profiles and sending out social media updates. I've actually outlined a lot of the uses and techniques in the other articles in the series, but many businesses still aren't using Hootsuite for social listening or prospecting or customer service - or any other number of possibilities.

Social Media Professors

Hootsuite seems very interested in partnering with professors and colleges to help educate college students who are looking for a career in social media and internet marketing. For professors, Hootsuite offers complimentary access to the University along with a number of additional materials and access. Professors are given sample curriculums and their own community.

Enterprise Teams

Hootsuite has a number of courses (listed below) that are specifically geared toward the Enterprise user. While social media managers as well as Enterprise Teams will use Hootsuite for many of the same purposes and goals, the introductions of Teams to environment adds additional levels of functionality and complication, like assigning tweets to other team members, having internal chats and conversations to determine official responses, and other advanced tactics. Making Hootsuite University available to all team members is a great way to ensure that everyone responsible for social media within the Enterprise are on the same page and have the same skill set.

If you're interested in jumping into an enrollment, you can start here (Hootsuite University costs just $21/month per user).

What Courses Are Currently Offered Within Hootsuite University?

Hootsuite Certification Courseware

- Getting Started with Hootsuite
- Advanced Tactics with Hootsuite Pro

Hootsuite Enterprise Training Courseware

- Hootsuite Enterprise for Team Members
- Hootsuite Enterprise for Admins
- Advanced Tactics with Hootsuite Enterprise

Social Media Courseware

- SCMD 110: Setting Up Your Social Media Profiles - *NEW Google+ Lesson*
- SCMD 115: The Dos & Don'ts of Social Media Etiquette
- SCMD 120: Introduction to Social Media Across an Organization
- SCMD 121: Introduction to Social Networks for Organizations
- SCMD 140: Growing an Online Community

Lecture Series

1. Social Network Specific Education

- The Google+ Playbook: Building Engagement on G+ Pages & Communities with Scott Wilder
- Brand Management using Twitter and Hootsuite with Twitter Representatives, Mark Stockx and Wendy Tapia
- How to Strategically Grow Your LinkedIn Network with John Hill from LinkedIn
- Do you have Klout? Understand and Grow Your Influence Online with Joe Fernandez, CEO of Klout
- Klout for Business: leveraging influence for your brand with Joe Fernandez, CEO of Klout
- 5 Best Practices for New Facebook Pages with Hootsuite University
- Relationships that Drive Results: 5 Key Steps to Engaging Followers on LinkedIn
- How the Best Brands Tell Stories Using Tumblr with Ari Levine
- Building a Powerful Community on YouTube with Ryan Nugent
- How to Amplify Your Paid & Earned Social Media with Storify
- Facebook Brand Pages: Rules of Engagement with Jason Li

2. Becoming A Social Business

- Securing Your Organization in the Social Era: An Approach to Social Media Governance, Guidelines, and Education
- The Shift to Social Business with Michael Brito, SVP of Social Business Planning at Edelman Digital
- The Redefinition of Traditional Media Models with Todd Defren
- Selling Social to the CEO with Greg Verdino
- The Collaborative Organization with Jacob Morgan
- The New Social CMO: 5 Ways Your Competition is Not Leveraging Social, Yet with Ian Wolfman and Mark McKinney
- The Business of Social with Matt Switzer
- Tips from the C-Suite: How to Build a Social Friendly Enterprise with James Amos and BJ Emerson
- Reorganize Your Social Business with Ben Watson

3. Social Media Best Practices

- A Guide to Content Curation: How Social Media Changed the Game

with Cameron Uganec
- Social Security: Protecting Your Brand Against Social Media Hackers with Mark Risher
- Tactical Tips & Tricks for Social Media Success with Josh Ochs
- How to Get Your Life Back: 4 Tips & Tricks on Effective Social Media Management with Susan Murphy
- Where Context Meets Content with Gary Vaynerchuk
- How to Use Social Video to Drive Results with Cameron Uganec
- Return on Influence: Personal Power on the Web with Mark Schaefer
- Science of Social Media: The Design and Engineering of Contagious Ideas With HubSpot
- 5 Decisions that Drive Extreme Customer Loyalty with Jeanne Bliss
- 5 Advanced Tactics for Engaging your B2B Audience with Gord Hotchkiss
- Elements of Perfection: A Social Media Case Study with Whistler Blackcomb
- The Palms Hotel Case Study Review with Josh Ochs
- Digital Defense: Online Reputation Management in the Digital Age with David Krejci, EVP of Digital Communications at Weber Shandwick

4. Social Media Education by Department

- Rethinking Recruitment: Building NPR's Employment Brand with Lars Schmidt
- The Social HR Imperative: How to Establish an Internal Social Media Philosophy & Brand with Ambrosia Humphrey
- 7 Steps for Sales Teams Going Social with Julio Viskovich
- Social Media for Event Marketing: 6 Tips to Boost Awareness & Attendee Participation with Lorien Henson
- Be Local Everywhere - Growing Your Online Community with Dave Olson
- Social and SEO: Two Peas in an Inbound Pod with SEOmoz
- Customer Service in a Social World with Sharad Mohan
- Streamlining Social Support: Turn Conversations into Value with Get Satisfaction
- How Small Businesses Can Stand Out and Hire the Best People with Don Charlton, CEO of The Resumator

5. Industry Specific Education

- 3 Steps to Social Success in Entertainment: How MTV's The Buried Life is Growing a Loyal & Engaged Audience with Penni Thow
- 7-Step Guide to Social Media Success in the Healthcare Industry
- How the Real Estate Industry is Leading the Way in Social Media
- Social Media Security & Compliance in Financial Services with Amy McIlwain
- Teaching Social Media to Digital Natives with Dr William J Ward
- Driving Admissions through Community Building: Best Practices for Higher Education with Inigral

What Other Benefits Are Included With Hootsuite University?

As you can see from the course list above, Hootsuite University offers more than just a few "How To" webinars on their tool. If that's all it was, I wouldn't be recommending it. The courses are very comprehensive and cover a wide range of social media topics, and include online testing for verification of knowledge.

The University also includes a Lecture Series featuring Industry leaders as you can see from the list above. Experts like Mark Schaefer and industry experts like HubSpot and SEOmoz are included, and Hootsuite is regularly adding new lectures to the list.

Anyone who completes the Hootsuite Certification Courses will be listed on the Hootsuite University site as a Certified Hootsuite Professional (as I am).

Students also gain access to Hootsuite's social media job boards.

What Are the Hootsuite University Courses Like?

So the real question many of you have is what are these courses actually like? It's one thing to read through all the benefits and course offerings - most of which you can get from the official website or brochure.

Most of the lectures are in this format, with a great slideshow presentation and voiceover dialogue from the presenting expert. Some utilize Google+ Hangouts, and all are presented within the Hootsuite University framework.

The courses include combinations of outlines, workbooks, videos, presentations and exams. The videos also include internal playlists so if you want to review a specific section, you can jump right to that frame.

Overall, they're very well done and extremely informative. Whether you're just getting started in social media, or have been doing this for years, I'd strongly recommend reviewing all of the courses and lectures.

At just $21/month per user, Hootsuite University represents a tremendous value to social media managers and professionals. Since it's a monthly fee, you can run through all the courses and lectures, or complete them in your own time. Enroll here.

Next, we'll get into how to measure social media ROI using Hootsuite.

How to Measure Social Media ROI Using Hootsuite Analytics

One of the complaints that I hear often regarding Hootsuite is in the area of analytics. The fact is, Hootsuite's dashboard has such a complete and advanced set of metrics that they're simply overwhelming. Rather than present users with a few canned reports, Hootsuite allows you to create the *exact* report that you need, including whatever data points you want to be able to review. These custom reports are then saved and generated on demand or on a schedule and emailed to you.

Because there are so many options in terms of what can be included in each report, Hootsuite has assigned point values to specific options and given users a specific number of points available to use to create reports. We'll get into the details of those points in a moment.

The key takeaway though is that Hootsuite offers a full suite of analytics that you can use to build whatever reports you need. You can keep regular reports saved and have information emailed to you weekly, or routinely delete reports and create new ones on the fly.

Let's walk through how to create your first report, and then we'll cover everything else there is to know about the point system, the various reporting options, and some analytics recommendations for businesses.

How to Create Your First Report

To get to your Analytics, click on the graph icon for Analytics in the left sidebar. This will open up the Analytics Dashboard.

If you don't yet have any reports set up, you'll see a large graphic in the main window to create your first report. In the left sidebar, you may also note a series of template reports you can use to quickly get started. They are:

- Twitter Profile Overview
- Twitter Engagement - Summary
- Twitter Engagement - Detailed

- Twitter Aggregate
- Facebook Page Overview
- Facebook Insights
- Facebook Aggregate
- LinkedIn Page Insights
- Google Analytics
- Ow.ly Click Summary
- URL Click Stats - Ow.ly

Now, if you haven't already connected your Google Analytics to your Hootsuite account, now's a good time to do that. By giving Hootsuite permission to access your Google Analytics, you will be able to incorporate key site metrics into you social media reports so that you can view performance side-by-side. Click on Google Analytics and then click on Connect Google Analytics. You will be asked to log into Google in order to authenticate your account. Once done, you will be able to incorporate any of the available Google Analytics modules into your custom reports.

Below the list of templates is the Reports menu that changes your main window view from All Reports to any reports that you're still building and are in Draft mode. There's also another button to build a custom report, as well as the option to create Labels for the various reports you have to help organize them.

When you click on Create Report, it will take you to the Report Builder and initially open the list of templates along with the option to create a Custom Report. Under the templates you will see point values, which we'll review in a moment. For now, click on Twitter Profile Overview.

Whenever you start a new report or choose to insert analytics modules, you will be prompted to make certain choices. In this case, our first decision is what Twitter account to use. You can also enter a Keyword to track, which you change later and will understand the relevance momentarily.

We start with the Twitter Profile Overview because it's a basic report that everyone should have set up in their Hootsuite account (assuming they *have* one or more Twitter profiles).

When the report draft comes up, you can edit the Title of the report, upload an image for branding, and edit the Details in the left sidebar. It's a good idea to edit the Report Title here so that, when viewing all of your reports, you can easily find and open this one. For instance, I edited mine to read, "Twitter Profile Overview - Mike Allton" so that I know it's for my @Mike_Allton Twitter account, and I created a second, separate report for @SocialMediaHats.

You will be able to access saved reports on the fly, but you can also set an email frequency in the left side for when Hootsuite will automatically generate and email reports to you.

This is one of the really convenient and powerful aspects of Hootsuite Analytics.

By customizing your report header and layout, and setting a regular schedule for running the report, you can let Hootsuite create and send you *branded* PDF reports that you can then share with your team, your boss or your client, depending on who you're running the report for. Social Media Consulting agencies who are managing social networks on behalf of clients with Hootsuite can really leverage this feature to make an outstanding impression. Reports can be set up and customized in advance, and Hootsuite can automatically send them out on whatever schedule you set.

Every report is made up of specific modules, so you can add, remove or edit the individual modules as needed. In this case, we have a module showing us basic Twitter account information like number of followers, followed by a graph showing how many followers have been added over time, followed by a list of our most popular tweets. When viewing reports live, you can adjust the date range in the upper left corner of the report to show you whatever data you're looking for. (Note that most reports will only go back 60 days, so get into the habit of running the reports you're interested in at least once a month so that you can save them.)

In addition to having PDFs emailed to you, you can also export data as a CSV, which is particularly useful if you want to track activity for more than 60 days. You can email direct from Hootsuite using the Share button as well.

Once saved, you will have your first report within Hootsuite! Congratulations! Before we get into some of the other templates and custom reporting options, let's take a moment now to review that whole Point system.

Understanding Analytics Points

As I mentioned before, Hootsuite offers such a wide range of reports and complex options that it would be unmanageable to have everything available and sending you emails with PDF attachments regularly. Instead, Hootsuite gives us an allotment of "points" which we can then "spend" on the reports and report modules that we want to see.

Some modules and report templates are free, while others have a point value to them. Points are spent any time you save a report (draft reports do not cost any points until they are saved).

While some documentation and comments have talked about an amount of points "per month", that has only led to more confusion so I do not refer to points that way. Depending on the kind of account you have (Free or Pro or Enterprise), you simply have an allotment of points. You can spend those points to create one or more reports, and when you're out of points, you cannot add any additional reports or modules. The reports that you've already "bought" remain for you and can be accessed at any time. If you remove a report or modules, their point values are returned to your account and you can create new reports or add different modules.

Free Hootsuite accounts come with 0 points so if you're on the free plan, you'll only have access to the free templates or modules.

Pro Hootsuite accounts come with 50 points, which offer a wide array of reporting options. Enterprise accounts include access to some levels of reporting and modules that are not available otherwise.

So, if you have a Hootsuite Pro account, you'll have 50 points to spend on analytics. You can set up a Twitter Profile Overview like we just did which uses 0 points. You can add a Facebook Insights report which uses 30 points, and a LinkedIn Page Insights report which uses 20 points, for a total of 50 points.

At any time, you can delete a report or delete specific analytics modules within a report and get those points back to be used on something else. So the perception that Hootsuite doesn't include reporting, or that you have to pay extra for reporting, is simply false.

Now, if the points that come with the standard Pro plan aren't enough for what you want to be able to see and have saved permanently, you can Add Points to your account. Additional points are added 50 at a time, and invoiced monthly or annually depending on your billing cycle. On the billing statement, 1 report = 50 points, and costs $50 per month, so each additional point is $1.

Hootsuite Analytics Options

Now that you understand the basics of creating a report, and have a feel for how the Points system works, let's dive into all of your options when creating reports.

First, the customization aspects cannot be overstated. In addition to being able to brand your reports by customizing the header (which can also be hidden per report), you can also add additional text as "paragraphs" wherever you need to. And then you can include whatever modules and profile data you wish, so although many of the templates are network-specific, feel free to mix-and-match as needed.

For instance, you could create one Monthly Report that included all of the elements of the Twitter Profile Overview, Facebook Insights and LinkedIn Insights in one PDF.

You can find report modules to add in the left sidebar, segregated by network, or by clicking on the Add Module button within the report and choosing from the list. Again, you will not "use" any points until you've saved a report, so you can slide in whatever modules you want to see how they'll look, though all data displayed will be sample data only. You won't be able to see actual metrics for your social profiles until you've saved and ran the report.

If you do find that you want to create multiple reports, whether for different networks or perhaps different campaigns, this is where the Labels in the left sidebar can come in handy. You can create labels for whatever you need, and then drag reports from the All Reports view to the label you want. Then, click on that label and you'll only see those reports.

If you want to email reports automatically, you can set a schedule of daily, weekly, bi-monthly or monthly. Additionally, if you share a report via email with one or more people, you can choose to have them automatically included in the scheduled emails by selecting the checkbox under the schedule.

Each time you add a new module, just as when we set up the initial Twitter report, there may be some module-specific settings to adjust. For instance, there are some great analytics modules within the Twitter section for monitoring keywords over time. Here, you would need to pick and choose what keywords or hashtags you wanted to monitor, and of course you could adjust these any time you wanted to. This is a one way to do keyword research, but it's also great for monitoring brand mentions or custom hashtag usage over a period of time.

Recommended Reports

So now that you know how to build and customize reports, what kinds of reports should you be building?

First, understand that there are a lot of fantastic analytics and metrics available that are only going to be useful for select groups. For instance, if you've set up one or more teams and have two or more team members working within the Dashboard, there are some *extremely* useful report modules you can set up that will show you at a glance what each of your team members have been up to within the given reporting period. You can also bring Google Analytics data into reports, which is great if you're using the tool to create snapshot PDF reports for an executive summary.

Second, I do think it is important to monitor follower growth on social networks, so utilizing the free templates or pulling those overview modules together into one report is a great idea. While Page Likes are far from being the most important metric for determining social media ROI (return on investment), an increase in follower count is certainly an indicator of recent social media success that should not be discounted.

Twitter

Similarly, we need to have a birds-eye view of how much engagement we're getting with our social media activity. This is where you'll need to spend some points, and if you're active on multiple social networks, you may need to invest in additional points or regularly rebuild reports. For instance, to see how you've done on Twitter recently, you're likely going to want to run reports on how many ReTweets and how many Mentions you've received over a given timeframe. Combined, those reports will consume 40 points.

The ideal Twitter report would then include the following modules:

- Profile Summary
- Follower Growth
- ReTweets
- Mentions

At a glance, you would be able to see over the past, say, week, how many new followers you gained, and how much engagement you received. If all you're looking for is a snapshot, that will give it to you.

With ReTweets and Mentions, you have options for Detailed versions of those modules which also include the tweets, in case you're curious, and those modules use the same points so you can build the same overall report if you wish.

Now to this, you can add some additional modules which will provide greater context.

First, add the Keyword Over Time module so that you can track tweet volume for your most important hashtag. If you want to track multiple keywords, but want to save your points for other modules, just add a Keyword Over Time module for each hashtag. I'm currently tracking #SocialMedia and #ContentMarketing normally.

Next, add some of the modules within the Click Stats group. These modules will help you understand how much traffic to your website these updates, specifically, generated. Consider using:

- Summary Stats
- Clicks By Region
- Top Referrers
- Most Popular Links

Now, if you're wondering why we want to see referrals from a Hootsuite report and why we don't just get that data from Google Analytics, you'd be asking a great question! You see, within Google Analytics, you can certainly tell how much traffic your site received from Twitter or Google+ or other sources. However, what you can't tell is how much traffic came to the site *as a direct result* of your own activity. When other people tweet out links to your articles and people click on those links, Google Analytics counts all of those visits as referrals from Twitter. But Hootsuite can show you specifically what your own tweets generated. Both perspectives are important.

We've now created a very thorough Twitter report. It used all 50 points, and is only for one Twitter profile, so if you have multiple profiles or want to see similar statistics for other social networks, you will need more points. But on the other hand, this report only took us a few moments to throw together, so perhaps it's not such a big deal to delete it and start a new one if needed.

Facebook

For Facebook, most of the report modules reflect data that is currently available via your Facebook Page's Insights. There is demographic information on your followers which can be extremely useful for understanding your audience and building targeted messages, but it's unlikely that you will need to see that report information each and every month.

What is of more value is the performance of your specific posts. The Per Post Metrics will tell you how your recent posts did, what kind of post it was (link, image, etc.), how many it reached and how much engagement (likes, comments, shares, clicks) that post received. This module only uses 5 points so you could include it with a couple of the Twitter engagement modules to create a great Social Media Engagement Report.

LinkedIn

If your business is active on LinkedIn and has a busy Company Page, monitoring that activity is certainly important too. However, for most businesses, Company Page updates are rarely seen or engaged by followers, so spending 10 points on the LinkedIn Company Page Engagement module is not worthwhile.

Google+

Currently, all Google+ report modules are available to Enterprise users only. But within that category are several modules that would enable you to measure engagement across posts by providing aggregate counts of comments, +1's and re-shares. You can also track follower count and Page activity in the report.

Since Google+ is my most important social network, personally, this is a feature that I am lobbying to make available to Pro users and will be sure to share the news when this changes.

Link Performance

One of the interesting features of Hootsuite Analytics and the use of Hootsuite shortened links is that you can monitor a specific link's performance. As a part of more advanced marketing campaigns, you can set up A/B testing with links and different parameters, and then create a custom report that will track that links performance over time.

Monitoring specific links is yet another way that you can track and measure how your own social media activity performed, as opposed to shares from other readers and followers of your content. You can create that shortened, ow.ly link within Hootsuite and then use that same link on whichever social networks you wish to track. You can also use this report to track links that you provide other referral sources, like ads or links within guest blogs and sponsored content.

Simply add the Click Stats module to a new report or any existing report, and plug in the shortened link you want to track. The best part is, there's no point value to this module so you can track *an unlimited number* of shortened links.

This is another important distinction and clarification about Hootsuite Analytics. Some have claimed that Hootsuite doesn't have the tracking capability that third-party link shortening services like bit.ly offer. And while setting up a new module for each link you want to track is certainly cumbersome, you obviously *can* track whichever links you wish.

For instance, once a month, I share a growing collection of blogging articles and content marketing advice to Google+. Such resource lists are extremely popular on that platform, and relatively easy to do. I created the list within Evernote, including Google+ formatting, and have a shortened ow.ly link for each article. I then set up a report within Hootsuite for each link and can tell at a glance not only how those links performed the last time they were shared, but also how they have performed over time!

So for your important campaigns and social media shares, be sure to use a shortened link and create a new Click Stats report so you can monitor performance of that link.

Armed with these reports, or a combination of these key modules, every business should be well prepared to measure and understand the performance of their social media activity across multiple profiles and platforms.

How to Extend Hootsuite Using Hootsuite Apps

The final area that we need to review within Hootsuite is the App Directory. The App Directory is the way in which Hootsuite can be transformed into an even more powerful tool for helping you and your business. There are nearly 100 apps within the directory that have been developed by third-parties and/or Hootsuite, designed to extend the capabilities of the Hootsuite platform. Most of the apps are intended to create synergy between Hootsuite and another web service, like MailChimp. Some of the apps are free, while some come with a monthly price tag from Hootsuite. And some of the apps are for services that have their own fees as well, so pay close attention to any potential costs involved.

To review the directory and add one or more apps, click on the puzzle icon in the left sidebar. That will bring up the directory, where apps are categorized by New, Featured, Premium, Free and Installed. You can also browse through All apps or search by name. Most apps are completely free. The Premium apps have either a fee from Hootsuite, or the developer, or both. If there's a charge from Hootsuite, each of those apps includes a 2-day trial so you can check it out.

If you see an app you wish to install, simply click on the Install App button and it will be loaded into your dashboard. Some apps are simply plugins that add additional capabilities to Hootsuite, while others give Hootsuite the ability to access additional data and for those, you will be prompted to add additional streams of information to a tab.

For instance, if you install the Nimble app, it will add a link to the Nimble Profile when viewing any user within Hootsuite. On the other hand, if you install the MailChimp app, it will prompt you to create a stream to monitor email campaigns and newsletters sent out.

With so many apps, and so many differences between how businesses might use Hootsuite and these third-party services, there are a ton of options here. However, the available apps can be grouped into some general categories, which may help you determine which ones interest you.

Extend Social Media Management

As we've discussed in a previous chapter, Hootsuite supports some very specific social media platforms such as Facebook, Twitter, LinkedIn and Google+. Using apps, you can extend Hootsuite to monitor and/or post to the following platforms:

- Pinterest
- YouTube
- Foursquare
- StumbleUpon
- Tumblr
- Flickr
- Wordpress
- Blogger
- Vimeo
- Reddit
- Viadeo
- Sina Weibo
- App.net

Add Customer Relationship Management

Businesses that are serious about using social media to drive sales need to use a CRM platform, and integration with Hootsuite is incredibly powerful.

- Nimble
- SalesForce
- SugarCRM
- Batchbook
- OFunnel for LinkedIn
- Simple Sales Tracking

Add Sales Tools

While we're monitoring our contacts and making sure that we're always in touch, there are a number of additional apps we can install to further improve the sales process.

- LeadSift - get more leads from Twitter
- Google Drive and Dropbox and Box - access sales documents and other Drive materials and share to contacts
- ChattBack - offer realtime business text chat for sales or customer support
- Evernote - send social media status updates to Evernote
- Marketo
- Kapost

Add Analytics

In addition to Hootsuite's extensive and customizable analytics that we just reviewed, the following apps can be added to further enhance the analytics available, or bring in additional information to be studied.

- TrendSpotter
- SocialBro
- Demographics Pro
- JustUnfollow
- Brandwatch
- Vidyard
- uberVU

Monitor Email Campaigns and Communication

Businesses can monitor newsletters and subscribers, incoming email campaigns, and integrate email contacts to enable closed loop social selling.

- MailChimp
- Gmail
- Constant Contact
- SurveyMonkey

Improve Hootsuite

Finally, there are a number of apps that simple add great functionality to Hootsuite. I've talked before about the Hootsuite Syndicator, which I use to feed in content via RSS feed that I can share to my social profiles. These make Hootsuite easier or more powerful and more efficient.

- RSS Reader
- Bulk Schedule with HootBulk
- Scoop.it!
- Storify
- Circulate.it

And there are even fun apps like SoundCloud for pure, personal enjoyment.

With more apps being developed all the time, the Hootsuite app directory is clearly an impressive place to find ways to further enhance your Hootsuite dashboard and streamline business processes.

How to Make the Most of Your Hootsuite Account

From posting and scheduling to analytics and more, we've covered a lot of ground. Congratulations on making it this far, sincerely! There are quite a lot of technical details in this book, and hopefully it will serve as a great reference for you moving forward.

But beyond the technical "How To" of using the Hootsuite Dashboard, there are even more important considerations to discuss. And this, I promise, will simply be the beginning of the conversation. Not only is Hootsuite an evolving and improving tool, but so is each and every social network. And each of us, personally and professionally, find different value and use and interest in social media.

So where do we go from here?

My true purpose in writing this book and presenting all of this information to you was to *hopefully* make the technology disappear. Instead of wondering how to schedule a tweet, I want you to be thinking about the best language to use or information to include. Instead of wondering where to look for conversations that are taking place, I want you to be diving into meaningful discussions and providing valuable insights to your fans and followers.

That's when you'll be making the most out of your Hootsuite account. Knowing how to bulk schedule or set up link parameters is cool and might be useful to some of you, but the real point - the **real value** - is when you're able to use Hootsuite without even thinking about it to educate, engage and entertain your followers and potential customers.

Appendix

As a resource to readers, here is a checklist for how you can use Hootsuite on a day-to-day basis. This checklist is also available as a PDF online at http://www.TheSocialMediahat.com/HootsuiteChecklist

Social Media Success Using
Hootsuite for 30 Minutes a Day

These are the activities that a business can do each day using Hootsuite, and spend just 30 minutes!

☑ Check Twitter mentions.

☑ Check Facebook comments.

☑ Check Google+ comments.

☑ Check Listening and Monitoring tabs for customer service and prospect opportunities.

☑ Check new Twitter followers and take a closer look at potential influencers.

☑ Check influencer Twitter lists and Google+ circles for key activity.

☑ Create and schedule business status update(s) for the day.

☑ Check RSS feeds in Hootsuite Syndicator for articles to queue up and share, as well as potential material for blog posts.

☑ Check reports

☑ Participate in a Tweet Chat

For more great tips on how to use Hootsuite for Social Media Success, head over to TheSocialMediaHat.com/Hootsuite!

How to Mention a Google+ Profile or Page using Hootsuite

To begin, start crafting your Google+ post you normally would, either from within the Hootsuite Dashboard using the compose dialogue box, or if you're on an article you want to share you might use the Hootlet Chrome Extension.

First, remember that Hootsuite fully supports Google+ formatting so you can write as much as you want, include paragraph breaks, and use the * and _ to make words and phrases bold and italic as needed. You can attach a link preview or share a full image and include multiple links within the post.

Whenever you're ready, insert a + symbol followed directly by the Profile or Page ID number. When the post is published, Google+ will automatically convert that to the clickable user or business.

For instance, The Social Media Hat has a profile ID of 106860584597630365429 and when I put +106860584597630365429 into a Google+ post I will be mentioning my brand Page.

The technique itself is pretty easy. Finding the ID of course requires a little more work.

Because there's no automated lookup, you will need to open Google+ in a separate tab and find the ID you want to reference. I'll explain how in a moment.

Of course, some of you may be wondering, if you have to get into Google+ to get this to work, why use Hootsuite in the first place?

The most likely reason would be to take advantage of Hootsuite's scheduling capability. Since Google+ offers no native scheduling options, if you want to craft your Google+ posts in advance and have them scheduled to go out later in the day or a future date, you will need to use a tool like Hootsuite to do it.

Another fantastic business use is the capability of content curation that

Hootsuite brings. Businesses who set up RSS feeds from trusted sources within the Hootsuite Syndicator are treated to a daily dose of new articles and stories. Finding one that would be interesting and helpful to your audience is pretty easy, and then sending that post to the compose field is a click of a button, so it would be convenient to be able to mention someone once in a while.

So let's review how to find that ID.

Finding a User ID

The easiest way to find someone's ID is to view their profile page within Google+ and look at the URL in your address bar. Unless they have a Vanity URL (which we'll cover in a moment), you will see their User ID as a long string of numbers within that URL.

Highlight the string of numbers only, and then paste that into your Hootsuite compose field directly after the + symbol to mention that user.

Finding a Page ID

Similarly, you can get the Page ID for a brand page by visiting that Page on Google+ and copying the ID number from their URL.

Finding a User or Page ID when they have a Vanity URL

Since more and more users and Pages are adopting vanity URL's, those ID numbers are being replaced by their names, like +MikeAllton or +TheSocialMediaHat. Unfortunately, using the vanity name will not work - we still need the ID number.

For this, check out the recent posts from the user or page. Right mouse-click on the date stamp for one of the posts and open in a new tab. This will open the post in a new tab and reveal it's URL, and you will see the user or page's ID number included as part of that URL structure.

Just as before, highlight the numeric sequence only and paste that into your status update.

Acknowledgements

To say that a book like this wouldn't be possible without the amazing help and support of a great many people is an understatement. To that end, I will try to acknowledge everyone who has had a significant role in making this book a reality.

First and foremost, I need to thank Hootsuite, not just for creating a great product worthy of being written about, but for being so supportive. Collin and Evan and others have been truly fantastic.

And a huge reason for the existence of this book is the response that many of you provided as I started to publish those first few blog posts. You, my cherished readers, provided me the motivation and inspiration to continue to write about and explore the dashboard.

Once I finished the initial manuscript for the book, it was my Tribe of peers and colleagues who were quick to read it and offer an incredibly valuable "first look." You helped confirm that this was a book worth publishing, and I can't tell you how much your support means to me. Stephan Hovnanian, Denise Wakeman, Mia Voss, Wade Harman, Les Dossey, Lynn Abate-Johnson, Jenn Herman, Peg Fitzpatrick and Jason T. Wiser - THANK YOU!

One tribe mate, colleague and friend who has been amazing is Jeff Sieh. Jeff in particular has been an incredible sounding board and inspiration, and even took it upon himself to create a fantastic teaser video for the book, Jeff Sieh style. (If you aren't familiar with Jeff's famous video trailers, look him up on YouTube.) Thanks Jeff! I'm looking forward to collaborating with you on many more projects.

The bedrock of my life continues to be my Family and Faith. My little girl and wife have been tremendously understanding and helpful as we rushed to the finish line of publication, and my wife even lent her considerable design skills to the creation of the book's cover and graphics. To them, I owe a great deal.

About The Author

Mike Allton is the CMO of <u>SiteSell</u>. Content Marketing Practitioner and Author, he has spent years learning and testing blogging and social media tools and techniques. He has leveraged that experience as an award-winning blogger at <u>The Social Media Hat</u>. Catch him online at <u>@Mike_Allton</u>.

Printed in Great Britain
by Amazon

46174732R00061